Designer's Dictionary 2

By Bruce T. Barber

Edited by Stephanie L. Corsbie

Published by
The Signs of the Times Publishing Company
Cincinnati, Ohio USA

International Standard Book Number: 911380-54-X

TO: Pat, Lisa, Peter and Bruce

Preface

Few ideas are totally original. Modern architecture imitates ancient buildings — artists and musicians are consciously or unconsciously influenced by their predecessors and contemporaries. Some manufacturers duplicate the designs of their competitors with few if any changes.

The practice of developing and maintaining a "morgue" or collection of reference material is common among designers and artists. In the 30 years since I began, I have accumulated fourteen file cabinets full of choice ideas. Designers Dictionary 2 might be considered an instant idea file, a compilation of styles and artistic approaches to all kinds of subjects.

I'm grateful to the hundreds of illustrators, photographers and corporate advertising designers who contributed to the book.

Bruce T. Barber

Contents

Animal Zoo

This section offers a wide range of potential for all kinds of visual merchandising, retail display, creative illustration, children's structures and toy design. It is also interesting to observe all of the excellent construction and graphic work being produced today for the large zoos, animal farms and theme parks.

For retail promotions, we suggest easy to construct bins, displays and merchandisers from animal shapes. Other motifs can be used in detailed or stylized form for banners, displays, bright colorful wall decor, backwall construction and counterfront cut-outs.

An entire children's department can be transformed into an animal jungle with lions and tigers, an ark for a doorway, and modern pachyderms as merchandisers. All kinds of real or artificial material can be used, such as palm trees, straw carpets, leather, fauna and feathers.

Live animals could add a touch of realism, including monkeys in large colorful cages. Gerbels and hampsters could live in an unusual glass sided house, built into the wall of the department. Actual song birds and possibly a talking mynah could complete the menagerie!

Many of the world's animals, birds and mammals have become extinct. This has sparked new interest in "natural habitat" zoological gardens combining the best work of designers and zoologists.

The San Diego Zoo and Wild Animal Park have done an exceptional job in this area. Their graphics are interesting and professionally produced. The illustration used on their brochures and their trademark, although realistic in approach, has a snappy graphic look. Another excellent example of this type of graphic work is the trademark shown for the Markham Zoo in Florida.

Master Eagle Family of Companies

WHY DOES HILLS OFFER HILLS® OWN BRAND PRODUCTS?

Hills has developed an ever-expanding program of Hills® own brand products. Formulated for high quality. And lab-tested for high quality. Lab-tested against leading national brands, where they exist, for truly comparable high quality.

But without some of the expenses of the big national brands. Like nationwide advertising. Or nationwide distribution.

Or other big national brand expenses.

So Hills® brand products are at Hills low prices ... *really* low prices. Every day, of course.

It's one more bold policy in action at Hills—to offer value, and to help save you a bonny lot of money. Whenever you shop.

When we put our name on a product, we put our reputation on the line.

Hills
THE ANTI-INFLATION DEPARTMENT STORE

Garden Village Plaza, South Cheektowaga

George Urban Blvd. & Dick Rd., Depew

Store Hours 10-10, Monday - Saturday 12-5 Sunday

Warning: Credit Cards Can Be Hazardous To Your Wealth.

TO OFFER TRUE HIGH QUALITY AT REALLY LOW PRICES EVERY DAY.

© Pitt Studios

© VOLK

The National Small Town Weekly
© Grit Publishing

The Frog of the Baskervilles

I was a 97 lb. tadpole.

Planet of the Frogs

There's a frog in your future.

Superfrog

The Frog of Monte Cristo

Dr. Strangefrog

The Ugly Frogling

© San Diego Zoo

© Markham Zoo

© 1979 VOLK

© 1979 VOLK

AZTECS, INCAS & MAYAS

The Aztecs were one of the most civilized and powerful groups in Ancient America. They occupied the Valley of Mexico from about 1200 A.D. until they were conquered by the Spaniard Cortez in 1521. They borrowed much of their culture from the earlier Toltecs, who lived in the region before them and from the advanced civilization of the Maya of Yucatan. To them we owe chocolate. They prized it so much that cocao beans were used as money. Religion dominated every aspect of their life with many human sacrifices and elaborate religious ceremonies.

Possibly the most famous Aztec symbol is the great Sun Disk. It contained the Aztec versions of world history, myths and prophesy. It is interesting to note that recent diggings beneath the plaza which supports Mexico City's great cathedral have revealed some unbelievable finds including a massive stone depicting the sacred Moon Goddess.

The Incas developed their civilization in South America along the Western coast and at its peak, from 1450 to 1532 A.D., their empire stretched for more than 2500 miles north to south. Centered in the Andes in present day Peru, its capital was Cuzco, 11,000 miles above sea level. Other famous cites included Machu Picchu in the highland and Pachacamac in the lowland.

The Incas worshipped Viracocha as the great creator. His assistants included the Sun, Moon, Thunder, Stars, Weather, Earth and Sea, and these symbols are repeatedly found in Incan Art.

The Maya, perhaps the greatest of the civilizations, built a remarkable empire in Central America, from 300 to 800 A.D. They were great leaders in the development of astronomy and arithmetic and were the only Indians in Ancient America to develop an advanced form of writing. Today, Mayan architecture and art are held in high regard all over the world. Mayans lived in present day Quatamala, British Honduras and parts of Mexico, including Quintanaroo, the States of Yucatan, Compechee, Tabasco and Eastern Chiapass.

© Dynamic Graphics

In 1840 the American, John Loyd of Stephens, rediscovered the Mayan ruins and started a reawakening of interest in the ancient cities of Tulum, Chichen Itza, Merida and the famous Temples at Tikal.

The stepped castles at Chichen Itza and the pyramids on the plains of Mexico provide dramatic graphic symbols for this subject. The symbols taken from the stela (sculptured monuments) provide additional decorative ideas and inspiration for design.

Designs from characteristic vegetation from the Peruvian coastal areas influenced many of the designers in Ancient Peru. They were used on bowls, water jugs and ceremonial vases. Motifs included cactus, marsh reeds and desert succulents.

Barton Brands Limited of Chicago, importers of *Montezuma Tequilla* have taken the design features of the Aztec sun stone and the Aztec warrior and incorporated them into their advertising and bottle labels. This is an effective use of stylization and design to produce handsome promotional pieces.

From the 20 symbols within the inner rings of the sun stone, the designers for Barton have stylized four symbols representing different days of the week. Xochitl, the flower, represents the last day of the Aztec week. Mazatl a horned animal symbolizes the 7th day. Quiahuitl symbolizes the 19th day and Atl is the water symbol for the 9th day. The 3rd day of the Aztec week, symbolized by a house is Calli.

©Barton Brands

© Barton Brands

11

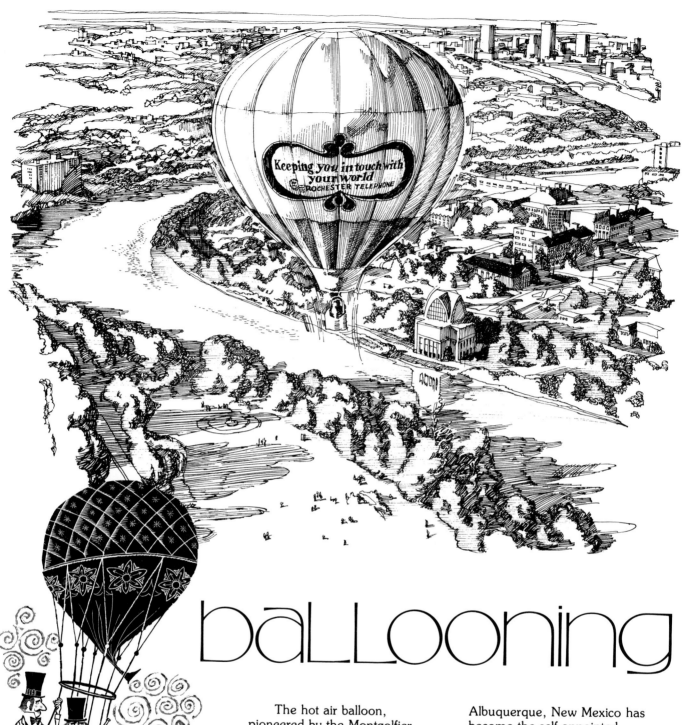

Keeping you in touch with your world
ROCHESTER TELEPHONE

baLLooning

The hot air balloon, pioneered by the Montgolfier brothers of France in the late 18th century, has enjoyed enthusiasm throughout the years. It has been used to carry observers aloft during wartime, such as the famous sausage balloons which were flown over England in World War II, trailing cables to trap enemy aircraft.

Development of the high capacity propane burner in 1945 launched the balloon into a practical sport that has grown in popularity ever since.

Albuquerque, New Mexico has become the self appointed balloon capital of the world with countless Balloon Fiestas and mass ascensions.

From a promotional standpoint, the hot air balloon has many possibilities as a symbol for retailing, display and advertising. Rochester telephone used one as a floating "billboard". The World Balloon Corporation features them as yet another way to transport vacationers on unusual trips.

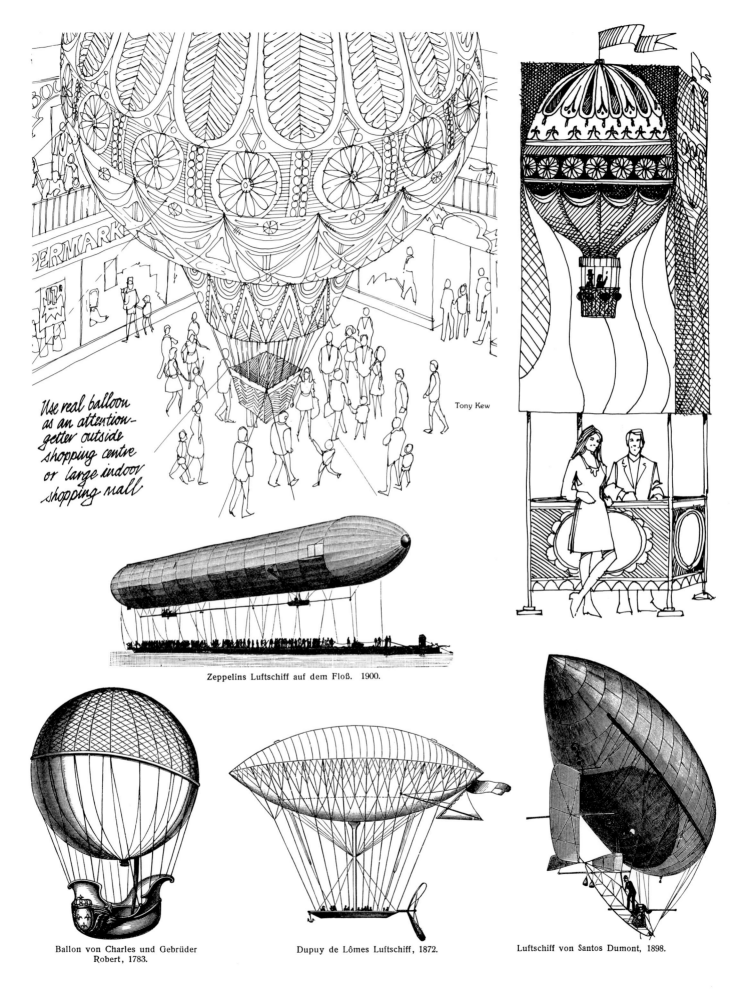

Use real balloon as an attention-getter outside shopping centre or large indoor shopping mall

Tony Kew

Zeppelins Luftschiff auf dem Floß. 1900.

Ballon von Charles und Gebrüder Robert, 1783.

Dupuy de Lômes Luftschiff, 1872.

Luftschiff von Santos Dumont, 1898.

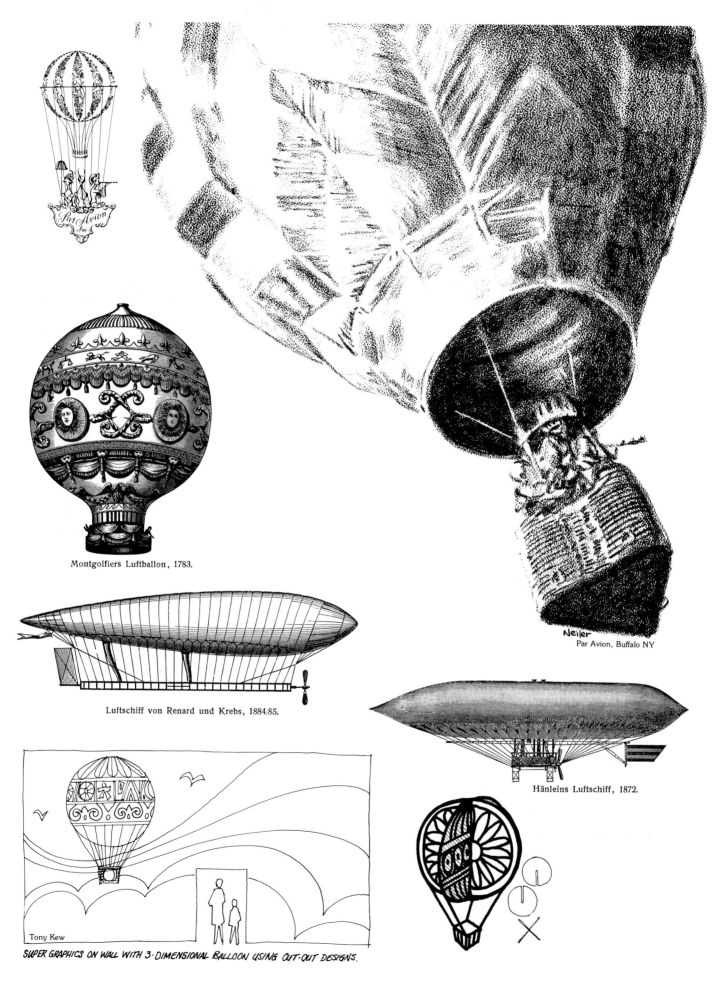

Par Avion
Inc

Neiler
Par Avion, Buffalo NY

Montgolfiers Luftballon, 1783.

Luftschiff von Renard und Krebs, 1884/85.

Hänleins Luftschiff, 1872.

Tony Kew

SUPER GRAPHICS ON WALL WITH 3-DIMENSIONAL BALLOON USING CUT-OUT DESIGNS.

14

Giffards Luftschiff, 1852.

INSTORE DUMMY BALLOON
SUSPENDED FROM CEILING

Tony Kew

THE BALLOON RANCH
at San Luis Valley
Star Rt., Box 41
Del Norte, Colo. 81132
(303) 754-2533

15

BASKETS

According to many display directors and merchandisers, "The world is basket happy right now." Baskets are an important decorative accessory that fits well into the current trend toward "natural" in texture, design, and color. The types, styles and sizes are numerous — Chinese lacquered straw, lunch baskets, some woven of clay, others made of flat reeds, splints and willows.

Baskets can play many roles in merchandising. First, the baskets themselves can be sold within the store. A full wall in one area can be converted into a charming boutique called "The Basket Barn." The exterior uses a carriage house hayloft construction with a mansard roof and a sign hanging from the block and tackle arm which protrudes from the loft. Baskets of all kinds can be stacked in front of the doorway, on open doors and even in a cart. The sales people can be appropriately attired in jeans and aprons, using the "BB" Basket Barn graphics.

Since basketry is a visually exciting craft, it might be advantageous to locate some live basketweavers and invite them to conduct demonstrations within the barn. In "The Shell Book of Country Crafts," James Arnold devotes a chapter to making baskets and traps. He states, "Basket makers sit very close to the floor, feet stretched out with a large board on the lap, on which their work is done. The variety of baskets they make and the techniques they use are varied and interesting."

Baskets can also be used for display and general merchandising. Throughout the store, you can establish basket bazaars displaying personalized gifts packed in all types of baskets. Booths can be created using awnings with baskets hung from them.

Tying in with the basket bazaar idea, the weave design can be incorporated into shopping bag motifs. In a special Christmas promotion called "Christmas in a Basket," each department in the store uses baskets to sell its own specialty items. For example, in the sports department, a basket for a tennis player might hold a pair of shorts, a hat, tennis balls and a towel. For the gourmet, a basket might contain a cookbook, a cutting board, measuring and mixing spoons, a wisk and a mitt.

Paul Taylor

Bavaria

Beer and ale steins are the symbolic cliche of Germany. This section contains one on each page — just to maintain the tradition.

As a design element they have great potential. The shape provides dozens of areas for decorative treatment and, because the steins carried symbols and paintings, it is only natural for illustrations of them to carry that decorative motif.

Dynamic Graphics handles the subject with a bold stylized technique. The Bavarian piece is a print from a 1890's decorative catalog. The fine line drawing incorporates the burgermeister's face, yodelers on a mountain and a pretzel motif.

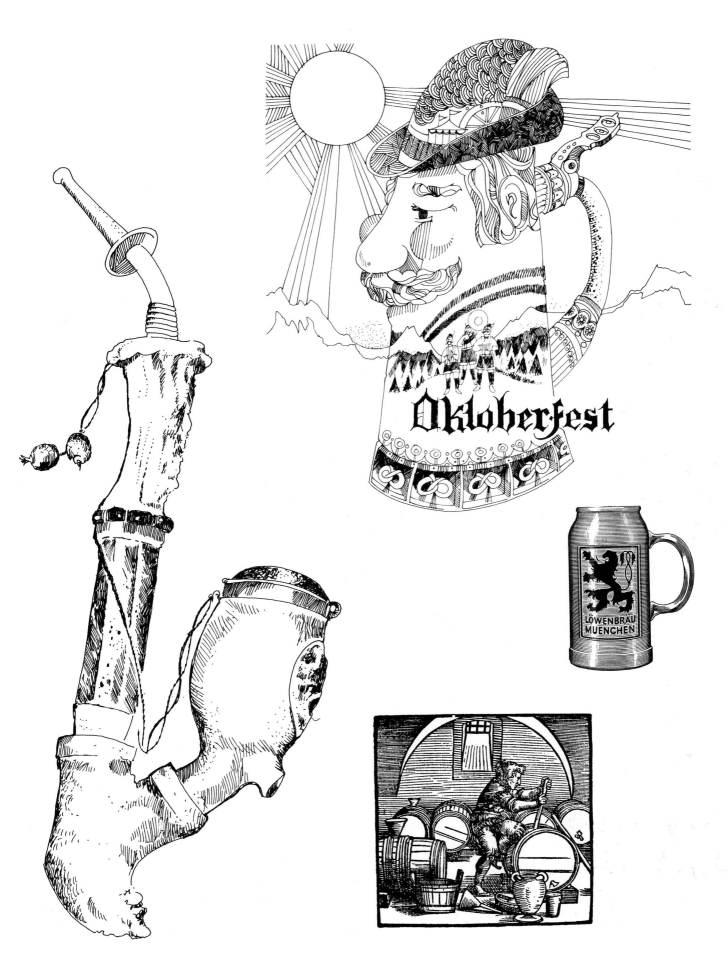

Oktoberfest

LÖWENBRAU MUENCHEN

Black Forest Smock

© Folkwear 1976

KAISER WILHELM.

© Dynamic Graphics

22

THE CALIFORNIANS

When using the adjective "dynamic", everyone agrees that California is loaded with it. In addition, this state is ideal for promotion, merchandising, graphics and symbolism. The California symbols selected to open this section are an orange slice, a palm tree, the Golden Gate Bridge and a cable car.

Years ago, as the Spaniards moved northward from Mexico and South America, they formed what is called El Camino Real, "The Royal Road". This trail of 21 missions that line the coast from San Diego to San Rafael was the beginning of the Golden State.

These monuments, with their unusual carved doors, arch shaped windows and bell towers, have tremendous potential for California mission style constructions. The roof cutaway shows how the two piece barrel

tile mission roofs are assembled. The drawing is from the Ludowici catalog, a famous manufacturer of old style mission tiles. Continuing the mission motif, the Franciscan pottery has used a simple three bell tower motif for their California craftsmen trademark.

When James Marshall found gold at Sutters Mill in 1848, he opened the flood gates to all kinds of expressions and advertising campaigns — The '49ers, Discover California, and The Gold Rush. The state flower is the golden poppy, which fits with the Golden Gate, oranges and the sun.

The city of San Francisco is difficult to characterize. It is a proud old dowager basking in moon glow at the Garden Court of the Palace Hotel, a Chinese dragon dancing down Grant Street, and Sicilians talking in Union Square. It is a labyrinth small enough to hold in your hand, but large enough to get lost in forever.

Because of its geographical location, San Francisco has a range of ethnic neighborhoods, from Chinatown to Little Italy. For the photographer, this city is an absolute kaleidoscope of views. For the retail merchandiser, it is a hundred and one exciting approaches to selling.

The town of Sausalito has unique charm. Its main street hugs the coast with a marvelous mix of boutiques, restaurants, hotels and shops. It offers a spectacular view of San Francisco across the bay. For sheer delight you can take the ferry between Sausalito and the Embarcadero, said by many to be one of the most beautiful boat rides in the United States.

Shown towards the end of this section is an example of a retail promotion developed around Pier 22. It is modeled

after the many shoreline pier houses found near Mendocino, north of San Francisco. The shop is in a twin unit building reached by a pier walkway. A huge sun symbol above the retailing spaces serves a graphic spot.

The motif is repeated in a twin sign, constructed of polished river stones in a curved base, with double poles and panels. An artichoke provides the design theme for a gourmet promotion called Epicurean Faire. Another design idea picks up the symbols in hanging mobiles for a store presenting "The Californians."

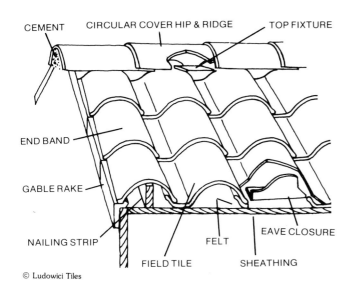

CEMENT
CIRCULAR COVER HIP & RIDGE
TOP FIXTURE
END BAND
GABLE RAKE
NAILING STRIP
FIELD TILE
FELT
SHEATHING
EAVE CLOSURE

© Ludowici Tiles

CALIFORNIA

SAN RAFAEL
SOLANO
SAN JOSE
SAN FRANCISCO
SANTA CLARA
SANTA CRUZ
SAN JUAN BAUTISTA
SAN CARLOS
SOLEDAD
SAN ANTONIO
SAN MIGUEL
SAN LUIS OBISPO
PURISIMA
SANTA INES
SANTA BARBARA
VENTURA
SAN FERNANDO REY
SAN GABRIEL
SAN JUAN CAPISTRANO
SAN LUIS REY
SAN DIEGO

California
Easy as Pie

Californian Caper

25

DISCOVER CALIFORNIA!

The California Craftsmen

© Franciscan Pottery

Macho Skateboards

27

Christmas

And suddenly there was with the angel a multitude of the heavenly host praising God, and saying, Glory to God in the highest and on earth peace, good will toward men. Luke 2:13,14

Design Quarter Tom Lewis

Best Wishes   Color Design '85

Christmas can take many forms. Like a Graham Sutherland painting, using Christmas shapes, in the form of stars, trees and ornaments as a stylized format or in the traditional forms shown throughout the following pages.

Christmas in American colonial times was heaped with heritage. A merchandising theme illustrated is called "Christmas in Nantucket". More colonial ideas are: a colonial hat with wig, an old tavern stage coach sign heralding "The Heritage Collection", and the Christmas pudding, a gift basket boutique sign for the holidays.

Sleighs have all but disappeared from the American scene. It certainly is a pity that these graceful vehicles, so widely used in the past, have been pushed aside by the automobile.

As a Christmas theme, sleighs and sleds lend charm and tradition to displays and merchandising. The variety is unbelievable — Grandma's chair sled, a farm sled, a Pennsylvania holtzpung, colonial cutters and maybe best of all, the good old

American Flyers that we used in our youth to "belly flop" down crisp white hills.

For retail promotions, large sleds can be used in windows, on top of counter islands and right in the aisles as merchandisers. The forms can be stylized for signs, cutouts and mobiles, silk screened on felt, printed on bags and imprinted as tags.

Charles Dickens was the chief historian of Christmas in England. His heart warming stories, rich in detail and description, evoke a nostalgic ring. In ancient England, small hawthornes were watered frequently to force them into bloom and all over the England Isle, Christmas came into being.

All over England, the lamp lighters, bell ringers, toy sellers and the carol singers are quaint reminders of the day when a coach pulled before an English Inn or a great house, to celebrate Christmas.

Tall hats, great coats, mufflers and gloves were quickly put away as the guests hastened towards their mugs of Christmas

cheer. Little meat pies were baked, tiny flutes were given to children and snappers, those paper tubes that we associate with birthdays were used by the British at Christmas time to make a loud noise and to provide exciting fortune telling from the little papers inside.

So many great Christmas traditions seems to have originated in England, especially the bringing in of the yule log. It is a tradition that has been highly romanticized and by the way still practiced in America, during Christmas time in Colonial Williamsburg. Few fireplaces today are large enough to accommodate the enormous logs that were once used. They had to be huge as it was expected to last from Christmas Eve until Epiphany. The Vikings introduced this practice in England, when their log was burned in the honor of the God Thor. It is customary to drag in a carefully selected log from the forest and ceremoniously place it on the massive hearth. A burst of song welcomed its arrival and everyone feasted in front of the

29

fire. Fragments left from one year's yule log were carefully saved, to be used for kindling the next year.

The Swiss, German and Austrian traditions reflect their bountiful culture and traditions. Germany is the home of many of our Christmas customs, such as the Gingerbread House. Martin Luther, who founded the Lutheran church, was the first person to put lighted candles on his Christmas tree. The candles represented the stars that shown on Bethlehem, when Christ was born. In Nurnberg, the toy center of Germany, are produced the fine pieces of tuned and hand crafted workmanship with delicate hand painting. A little tinsel angel, often called the Christ child of Nurnberg, is the traditional top ornament of the German tree. People from all over Germany flock to the toy city to attend the annual Christkindl Market.

Another Swiss German sweet, Marzipan, is symbolized in the heart and angel shapes. In Rumania, one of the most charming holiday sights is the procession of young boys with a six point revolving star in the form of a lantern, gathering at dusk to go through the streets, stopping at each door and singing old carols about the star that shone above the stable at Bethlehem. The star is duplicated in cookie forms and another traditional cookie is made in the form of the mushroom. Apples are another important symbol of the Scandinavians. Place fat sheafs of wheat tied with a bright ribbon in the corner of each room to symbolize the harvest. The sheafs also become a gift to the birds at the end of the Christmas festivities.

In old Russia, it was Babouschka who brought the gifts to the children. She was the counterpart to the Italian Befana. In the early days, a white robed maidens, known as Colyada, was driven in a sled from house to house on Christmas eve and

the young people attended her with songs and they, in turn, were rewarded with gifts.

Each country had its own traditions. From Holland came Sinterklass, Dutch for St. Nicholas, in Germany it was St. Martin and in Greece it was St. Basil. The Vikings had their own Julesbukk in the form of Thors goat. In 1605, notes were found to substantiate that this was the year that made first reference to the Christmas tree. The mixing and intertwining of all of these traditions and beliefs present themselves now in every country around the world.

SEASON'S GREETINGS

Forstall Typographers/The Ad Shop • 1201 South Rampart Street • New Orleans, Louisiana 70153 • (504) 524-0822.

Design Jim Bonner Advertising Art

© Forstall Typographers

HOLIDAY

© Fortune Magazine

Walter Wells

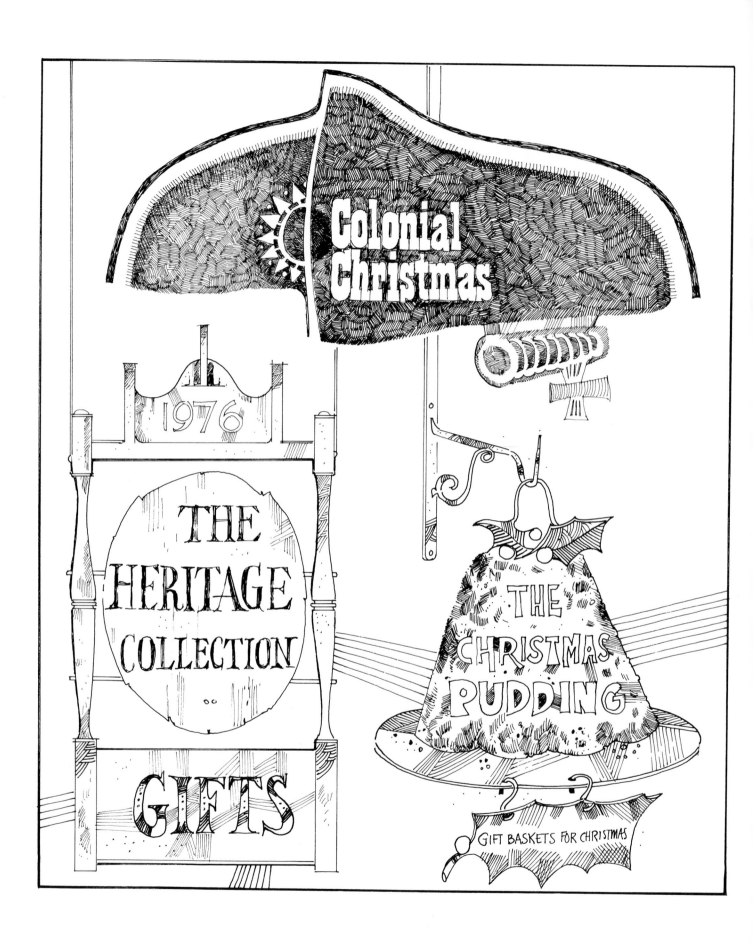

© Naiad Einsel

CHRISTMAS
ON
NANTUCKET

© R. H. Macy artist Walter Einsel

37

38

©VOLK

© Fortune Magazine

m.Stasolla

© David and Averil Walker

CIRCLES

Alka Seltzer
altimeter
axis
ball bearing
balloon
barrel head
baseball
basket
basket ball
beach ball
bike tire
billiard ball
bowling ball
bolt end
bow
bracelet
bread
bubble
button
cake
camera lens
cartwheel
cheesewheel
circular stairs
Christmas ornament
circus ring
clay pigeon
coaster
coconut
cog
coil
colander
column
compass
computer spool
cookie
cookie cutter
cup
curling stone
cutting blades
cyclorama
doughnut
dime
drums
earth
eye
ferris wheel
film reel
flower
french horn
frisbie
glass
globe
golf ball
grapefruit
gum ball
hamburger
hat

hula hoop
jet engine
laurel wreath
lazy susan
lemon
lollipop
manhole
marble
merry-go-round
mill stone
moon
mug
o (in the alphabet)
olive
onion
orange
peacock
perimeter
pie
pinwheel
pipe
pizza
pomegranate
potters wheel
porthole
propeller
pulley
pumpkin
raindrops
record
rings (of all kinds)
rope (in a circle)
rose window
round house
salami
saucer
shell
sleigh bell
snowball
snowflake
spool ends
stonehenge
sun
sundial
tambourine
target
tennis ball
token
tomato
tractor
traffic circle
Tums
wagon wheel
watch
watermelon
winners circle
wood tree slice
world, etc.

Of all of the standard shapes, circles are the most adaptable to all kinds of design applications.

The use of them is so varied that it would take a tremendous amount of space to completely explore the possibility, but these suggestions will be a starting point. The Aztec sun stone and the circle designs in the Californian section show the great possibilities.

From a graphic standpoint, the circle and the symbol contained in it can be detailed or stylized and for retail visual merchandising, the shape lends itself to many different areas and possibilities. In-store promotions can carry the circle format throughout, bolt or spool ends for the fabric department, cheesewheel, watermelon or pizza shapes for housewares and gourmet foods, snowball, marble or pin wheel for the children's department, etc.

The following are some suggestions and we are sure you can double or triple this list by yourself.

44

STAR of INDIA

BALBOA PARK

BEACHES

SEA WORLD

SAN DIEGO SAN DIEGO SAN DIEGO SAN DIEGO

ZOO

HOTEL CONVENTION AREA

MISSION

CORONADO

Cities

The fascination in this section is the diversity of approaches used by various cities' convention and tourist bureaus to convey the feeling of their individual community.

A montage of important symbols best illustrates Boston's unique style. There are line drawings of the Philadelphia skyline and a couple sites in Atlanta. Dallas and Washington, D.C. chose to promote their historical landmarks. The section ends with Norman Baxter's exquisitely detailed aerial views of two Southwestern American cities.

Philadelphia Economic Development Corp.

Hotel Triumph Sheraton, Toronto, Artist Tony Smith

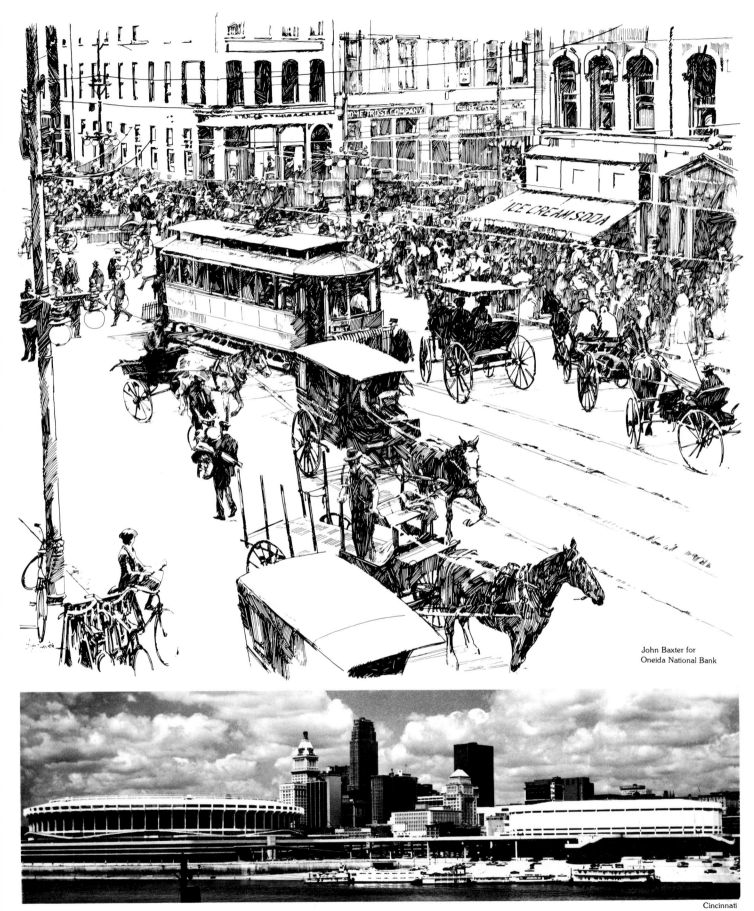

John Baxter for
Oneida National Bank

Cincinnati

48

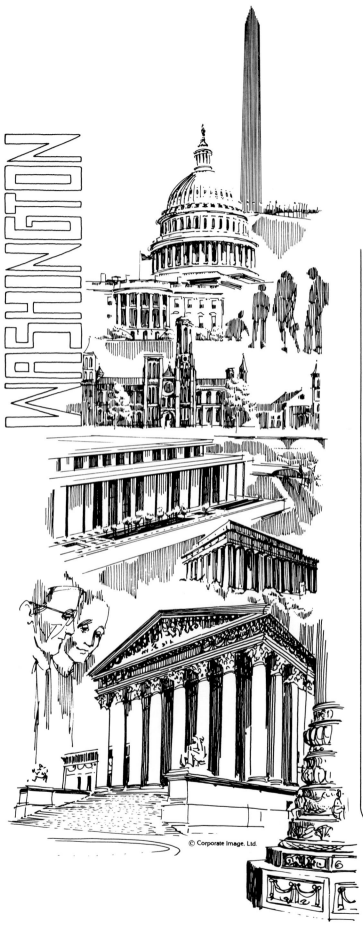

Old City Park

A Museum of Cultural History

A unique living history museum of restored 19th century buildings and their furnishings . . .
. . . an exciting slice out of Texas' colorful history.

Dallas County Heritage Society

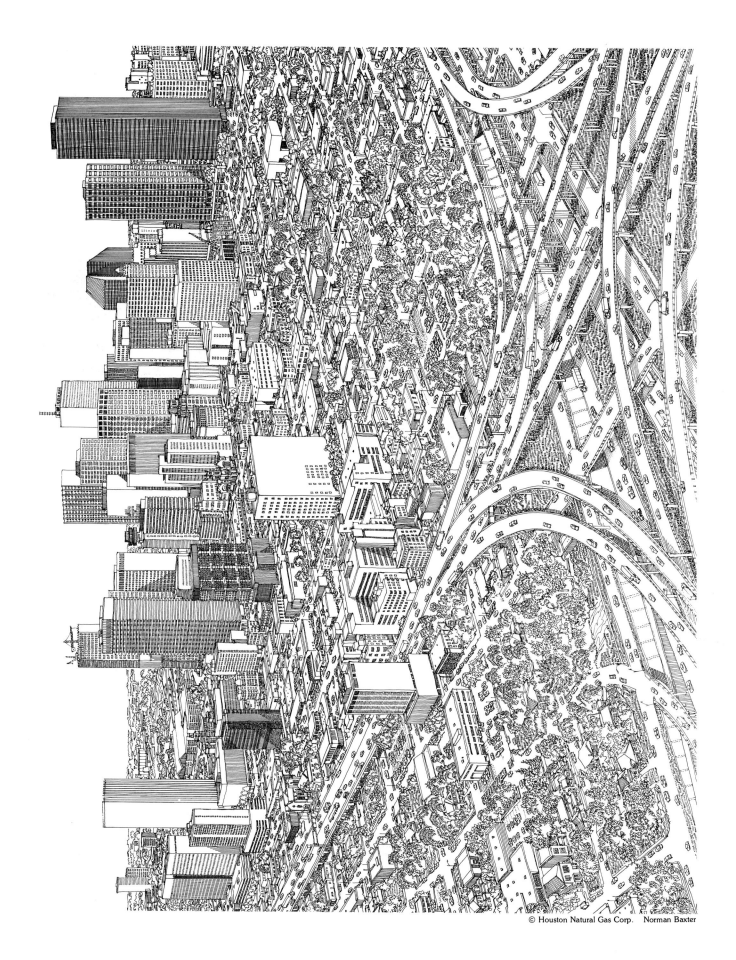

50

BOSTON

(c) CI/aia

Atlanta Convention and Tourism Bureau

Frontier Airlines

VANCOUVER

Southland Corp., Dallas

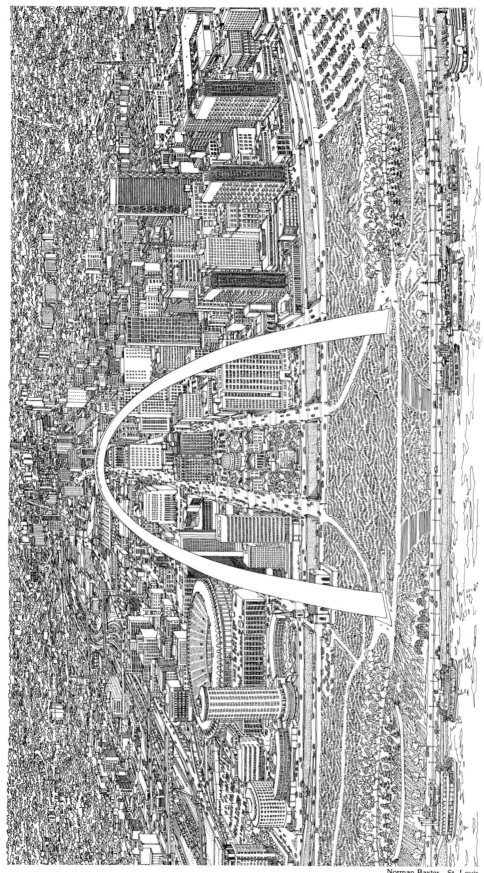

Norman Baxter St. Louis

52

Clip Services

As they say in the trade, "a lot of water has gone over the dam" since the first clip art services were launched. The quality level of these major sources of artwork has risen significantly in recent years.

Harry Volk (Pleasantville, New Jersey) was the pioneer in pure clip art. His work has always been high quality - current and provocative, using techniques that change with the times. His monthly subscriptions come in the form of 5½" x 7" subject clip booklets.

Association Image Art (Rockville, Maryland) is listed as an art component system designed exclusively for associates. It serves national associations with custom art studio work and graphic consultations. City themes are original two-color illustrations depicting major points of interest in "convention cities," Association Themes artwork covers membership campaign and report projects. Other artwork and designs are available for covers, certificates, and mastheads.

Forward Graphics (Des Moines, Iowa) offers a full range of black and white clip art, two-, three- and four-color separated pieces, and many other graphic services.

The Board Report (Harrisburg, Pennsylvania) is a graphic artists monthly newsletter service covering Trademark Trends, lettering, studio layout ideas, printing and production reports, and items of general interest. The service is available through an annual subscription with issues sent monthly to be placed in a special ring binder. Other large corporations, especially those involved in commercial travel and leisure, offer some clip art. United Airlines and American Airlines make sheets available through local sales offices, which are to be used in connection with their advertising.

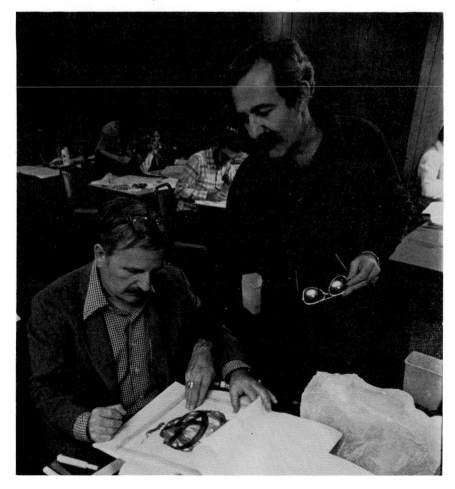

Dynamic Graphics (Peoria, Illinois) is the largest firm of this type. Their Clipper Creative Art Services(R) is both an art service and a creative idea source. It is published monthly on a subscription basis. Each issue contains suggested layouts for ads, brochure and booklet covers, posters, calendars, newsletters and other designs. There are also seasonal and thematic designs by nationally known artists. The camera-ready art is primarily black and white line, and easily enlarged, reduced, cropped, reversed, screened or converted to two or more colors. A full-color separation is also included each month. A magazine supplement to Clipper(R) is "Clip Bits", which provides "how-to-do-it"

articles, tips, tricks of the trade, and current examples of how other subscribers are using the Clipper art.

PMS(R) or Print Media Service(R) is a companion service to Clipper Creative Art Service. It provides retail and publication oriented art all in finished form with contemporary headings, borders, text and logos in position. Two copies of PMS and its magazine supplement "Tearsheet" are sent to subscribers each month. This enables users to keep one issue in their master file and work with the other on current projects.

The Dynamic Graphics Bookshelf is a ready-reference library of contemporary publications of interest to the graphic designer. The books

generally fall into three broad categories - idea sources, technical and "how-to" books for the novice. A number of management-oriented books are also available. The Dynamic Graphics Bookshelf catalog is published three times annually.

The Dynamic Graphics Educational Foundation seminars are specifically designed to upgrade skill levels and knowledge of the professional designer as well as the novice. Focus of these results-oriented programs is on practical, hands-on instruction. The seminars range from 2 to 5 days in length and cover specific areas in graphic design and management. The seminars are offered at strategic locations throughout the country.

COUNTRY

The material in this rather large section came from many sources. It starts with some illustrations from the Vermont Bean Seed Company, who sell virtually every variety of beans and pea seeds available. The beautiful sketches were done by several New England artists for the Vermont Bean Seed Company and appeared in their 1979 catalog.

The photograph on page 58 was taken from an article by Margaret Clayton called "A Journey into the Past" that appeared in a 1976 issue of Woodalls Travel Trailer magazine. It reviewed her discovery of Patterson's Mill Country Store in the Durham/Chapel area of North Carolina. Surprisingly enough, this bit of nostalgia was built only a few years ago by John and Elsie Booker. They used 19th century floor plans, as well as original lumber and fixtures. The result is this charming store museum that looks so authentic, it has been used in several television commercials.

By way of historical background, the old country store flourished during the period from 1860 to 1910. It played an important part in the lives of every family in the surrounding area. The country store was a common gathering place, especially for a game of checkers or cards. The proprietor wore many hats — he often served as postmaster, town clerk, justice of the peace, and perhaps even parttime veterinarian.

Every inch of space in the store was utilized, including the ceiling. Cumbersome tools and hardware were often displayed from ropes and chains. The candy counter was one of the most popular areas, and choices for a penny became a major life decision ("two-fers" and "three-fers" were bestsellers). Children's items ranged from knives for the boys to bisque head dolls for the girls. Characteristically, the old country store carried a somewhat strange assortment of products — chocolate, kerosene, onions, molasses, gun oil, yard goods, dry cod fish, sweet pickles, rubber boots, cocoa, coffee, wrapped cheese, pickled herring, cookies, tobacco . . . the list is endless.

A country store appeals to all the senses. The most important is sight — hanging pots and pans, country hams and old tobacco signs. On the shelves and counters are richly designed tins and boxes, kerosene lamps, button holders, spool cabinets, and a wide variety of nostalgia. Next is the sense of smell — freshly ground coffee, the scent of smoked bacon and aged cheese, oil for lamps, open barrels of pickles, and tin dispensers for cinnamon and allspice. Last, but not least, is the sense of sound — leather boots on hardwood floors, the slamming of a screen door, the low murmur of voices as people scurry about, cutting dry goods and chatting around the stove.

For promotions and graphics, it can be difficult to choose among the many possibilities. Cash registers are so rich in detail that they could stand alone as the identifying symbol for an old store. A theme can be built around a general store sign and shelf backdrop with old fashioned bins and compartments. It can include items such as brass front store bins, hanging lamps, lanterns, old clocks, glass jars, milk pails, bushel baskets, barrels and nostalgic graphics. Barn boards can be used as a background material, with actual pegged hardwood floors to add authenticity. And what could be better than old advertising antiques used as an entrance sign? Ready cut letters of all types are available, and small collectibles can be attached to the standard colonial type wooden signs.

Bernard Ethier

Stoves

This section contains a page showing the various types of stoves used years ago — massive ones, tiny "Swedish" ones, pot-bellied stoves, and old kitchen ranges. Cast iron was the basic material, with small sheets of mica for windows. Some had beautiful tiles, others had magnificent doors and ash trays.

The recent energy crisis has renewed interest in these old fashioned stoves. People who inherit one from Grandmother or find one buried in the back of a country store are extremely lucky.

Lunchpails

An old enameled lunchpail, with its wooden handle and somber grey granite finish, recalls long days in a one room schoolhouse under the watchful eyes of a stern schoolteacher.

These lunchpails and buckets were used for many things, including berry picking and keeping cream cold in the spring house. Around the turn of the century, buckets were used for "rushing the growler." Children were sent to the local tavern to buy ten cents worth of beer, which was carried home in the bucket and drunk at the dinner table.

Currently, authentic lunchpails are highly collectible, so if you find one, treasure it.

F. Allyn Massey

Barns

Students of architecture and "barn freaks" worry that barns are an "endangered species" and might disappear entirely. This would be a great aesthetic loss, since nothing can match their deep brown beauty and structural grace. These buildings have a rich heritage,

ranging from the English and Dutch barns to the now famous Pennsylvania barn. In the East, the Shakers even constructed some in fascinating circular and polygonal forms. Movements to preserve and protect remaining barns have been started.

In 1875, eighty-five percent of the population of the United States and Canada lived on farms. Barns were a vital part of rural life because they held the harvest of summer, food for the cattle and work horses through the long winter, wagons and tools to work the land. To a farm family, the barn was *the* central structure.

Through the years, most barns became weak and eventually fell down or burned to the ground as a result of lightning or internal combustion. Barns are indeed disappearing, but some consolation can be taken from the fact that their forms have begun to resurface in contemporary homes. The shed roof and other geometric constructions are closely derived from barn architecture. Many firms specialize in producing homes and shops using barn construction techniques. Barn Homes Ltd. in Woodstock, New York, serves this market with a variety of styles. Their packaged homes (the wall and roof sections are prefabricated) retain the quality and building principles used by 18th century farmers.

The merchandising potential of the barn concept is very broad and can incorporate aspects of rural life such as wagons, pitchforks, and chickens. The hayloft idea illustrated is a suggestion for a small boutique, using a stylized wheat symbol, rough field stones and barnboards for atmosphere.

Two excellent books are available for reading and inspiration — **The Age of Barns** by Eric Sloanes (published by Ballantine) and **The Barn, A Vanishing Landmark** by Eric Arthur and Dudley Whitney (published by arrangement with New York Graphic Society, Ltd.). The latter is an amazing reference guide and probably one of the most educational books ever written on the subject.

Bernard Ethier

PURPLE POD

EXTRA EARLY

Leslie Bates

HARDY

BEANS AND PEAS

VERMONT BEAN SEED Co.

SEEDS

LARGEST
BEAN & PEA SEED
SELECTION
IN THE WORLD

Sandy Reiber

Prolific Easy Picker

Sandy Reiber

DWARF TELEPHONE

PEAS

VERMONT BEAN SEED COMPANY · DWARF TELEPHONE

HIGH YIELD

TOP CROP

Sandy Reiber

Forward Graphics

58

Pitt Studios

L.TAYLOR

Hooks Drug Co.

60

Morton Salt Co.

© Dynamic Graphics

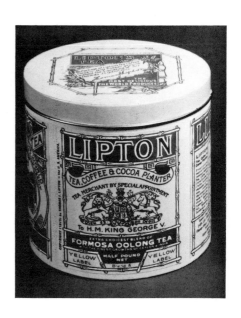

Cheinco Housewares

63

BARNS

Paul Taylor

Paul Taylor

© Pitt Studios artist L. Taylor

© Texas Festival - E.W. Forbes

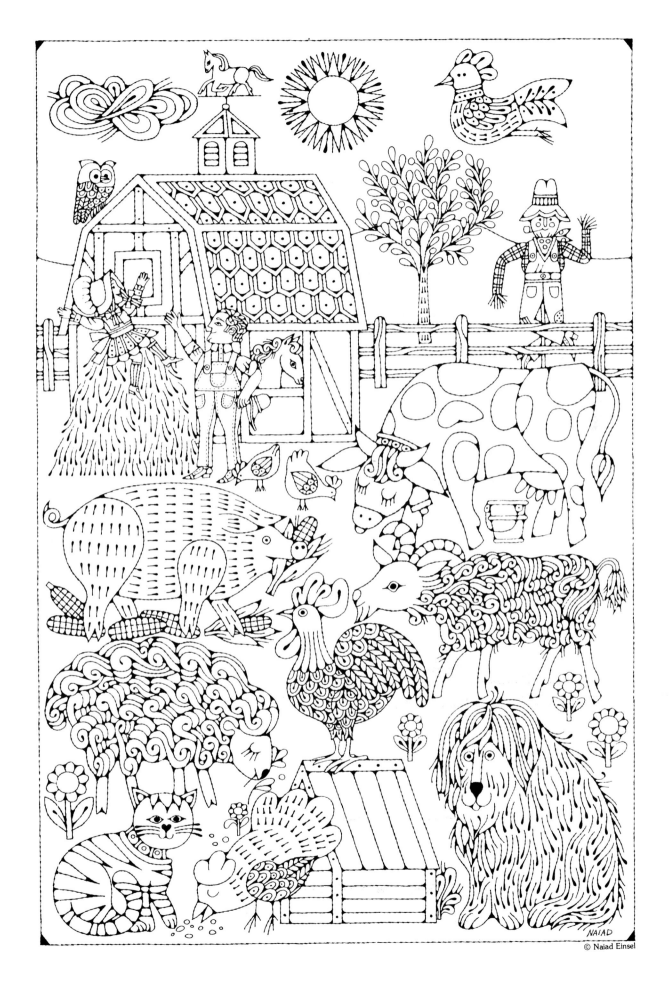

NAIAD

© Naiad Einsel

71

EGYQT

The Cousteau Odyssey

Now that the dust has settled (no pun intended) after the exciting American/Canadian tour of the treasures of Tutankhamen, we can reflect on the impact of those objects and how much they influenced the design scene.

The images and motifs offer countless possibilities for decorative applications, jewelry designs, retail display and merchandising.

Cartouches were used to outline the complete name of a King or Queen, and in the case of King Tut, his tomb contained a double case in the form of two cartouches. Solar discs, pomegranates, lotus flowers, Udjat eyes, falcons, beetles and Nile sailing ships are a few of the ideas presented.

Atlantic-Richfield Company sponsored the Cousteau Odyssey — exploring and researching the beginnings of the Nile, then continuing down the great river to its delta and out to the sea at Alexandria.

Egyptian Shirt

© Folkwear

Antony & Cleopatra

© Naiad Einsel

England has been termed a toy country of thousands of neatly painted houses, with millions of small polished windows shining after the rain, and countless green fields and beautiful woods. It is amazing that an island 600 miles long and 300 miles across (at its widest) should become one of the wealthiest and most powerful countries in the world.

The following pages of illustrations represent England. We start with Stonehenge, that mysterious circle of huge stones standing on the Salisbury plain in southern England, a monument older than the nation. These stones survive as a cryptic symbol of the remote past.

Next we go to the Globe Theatre, the home of William Shakespeare and his players, the Lord Chamberlain's men. It opened as a public playhouse in 1599 in Southwark, was burned in 1613, rebuilt in 1614, and finally succumbed to the wreckers in 1644.

Dr. Samuel Johnson once said, "There is nothing which has yet been contrived by man, by which so much happiness is produced, as a good tavern or inn." If ever there were a constant symbol of Britain, it would be the pub or country inn. Today, most of the pubs are owned by breweries, who thereby control the sale of their total production. The trade names are well-known in beer drinking circles: Whibread of London, Courage of Reading, Bass-Charington Ltd. and Arthur Guinness Son & Company Ltd., both of London, and John Smith's Tadcaster Brewery Ltd. in North Yorkshire and Watneys.

No one knows who put up the first pub sign, but it was a common practice among the Romans. Signs were found at Pompeii depicting a checkerboard, which was the emblem of a moneylender. In 14th century England, Richard III made it mandatory for proprietors of taverns to display signs. They were designed mostly for people who were illiterate, as the only way of showing a trade. In those days all traders used signs, and as competition increased, the signs became more elaborate.

The artwork depicted on those signs carried the pub name, of course, and many had beautiful oil paintings of animals, people, elaborate scenes, heraldry, trains, humorous pictures, and even Adam and Eve. It is interesting to note how one animal or subject can produce a proliferation of pub signs: the Bear and Bells, Bear and Swan, Bear's Head, Bear's Paw, The New Bear, Two Bears, The Cat and Fiddle, Cat and Mustard Pot, Tabby Cat, Kicking Donkey, Green Dragon, Rocking Horse, The Brown Lion, Lion and Unicorn, Grey Ox, Blue Pig, Sow and Pigs, Stag's Head, etc. The list is endless and covers almost every subject. Many are devoted to knights and warriors of old, and some ladies - Nellie Dean, The Three Connies and Percy Erms. There are also sporting signs - The Checquered Flag, Speedway Tavern, and The Yorker.

Recently, there have been grumblings that pub signs are being mass produced. However, many breweries still maintain their own art staffs, with Watneys and Courage having some of the largest studios.

The buildings themselves are as varied as their names. Pubs can be found in tiny thatched houses, in beautiful country farm houses and on side streets in the largest cities and small towns.

The remainder of the work in this section includes London Bridge, Big Ben, castles, kings, queens, crowns, and other royal symbols. Last but not least is Henry VIII.

Barbican Centre

Freelance Photographers Guild

LAWSON

W. WASHINGTON

Freelance Photographers Guild

© Texas Festival - E.W. Forbes

82

Queen Victoria & Albert

© Naiad Einsel

VICTORIA · REGINA · 1837 · IMPERATRIX · 1897

VICTORIA

Freelance Photographers Guild

© Dynamic Graphics

83

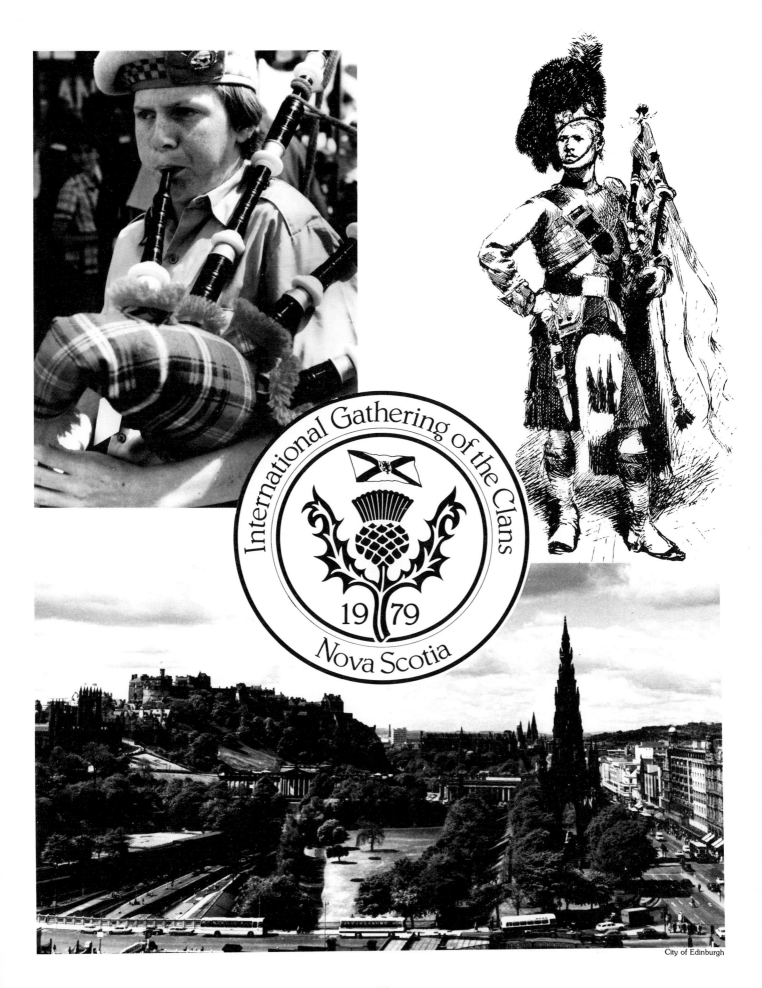

International Gathering of the Clans

1979

Nova Scotia

City of Edinburgh

© Texas Festival — E. W. Forbes

Houston Coca-Cola Bottling Company, Conroe Division

The First Americans

Mead Printing & Writing Paper Div.

It is encouraging to see renewed interest in the American Indian, as the fact remains that "the Indians were here first". Most local histories begin with a chapter on American Indian life as it relates to that particular region, town or city. Indian life and customs were used as basic material out of which we fashioned a national identity, even before our Independence was declared.

To view major collections of Indian clothing, saddles, medicine bundles, masks, war bonnets, etc., is to experience a revelation of how unique and artistic these first Americans really were. Pottery from the Acoma Pueblo and Crow Indian bead work saddles can be ranked as some of the greatest craftwork ever produced. We think you will find trips to the major Indian museums and collections in national museums to be time well spent and completely rewarding.

The Rockwell-Corning Museum in Corning, New York, has an outstanding collection of Indian relics, artifacts, art and pottery devoted to all aspects of the life of the American Indian. This excellent museum is connected with the Corning Glass Center and has become a mecca for both students of the American Indian and glassware from around the World.

Keith McConnell "Wooden Lance"

Shawmut Bank of Boston

T. YEATES
1977

Koh-I-Noor

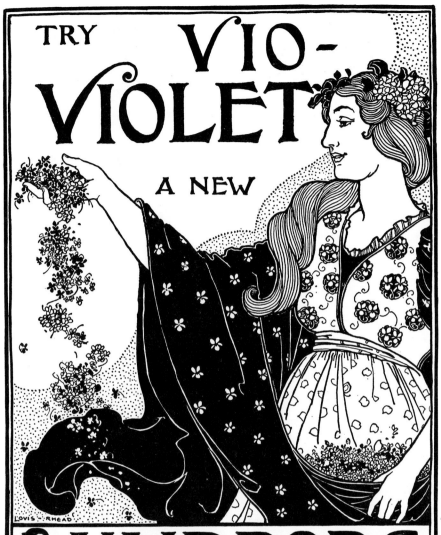

FOOD

This is a diverse subject, and covers many aspects and approaches of merchandising, display and advertising. The section opens with a page of strawberry illustrations.

Coffee and tea shops, stores and specialty departments have sprung up all over the country. Renewed interest in these traditional beverages has boosted sales of firms like First Colony, along with books devoted to the products, published by houses like Potpourri Press in Greensboro, North Carolina. Promotional tie-ins of coffees and teas in restaurants are also growing.

The wide range of food illustrations is emphasized in the examples shown. George Stavrinos, widely known for his fashion illustration, is represented with a fine drawing for the New York Times Magazine. The Richards Group illustration for the Faneuil Hall ads (another appears in the Malls and Markets section) is a tasteful example of grease pencil on canvas.

Canning has become extremely popular of late. A merchandiser could be made in the form of a fruit jar with glass shelves to hold canning jars, strainers, cooking pots, and other equipment. The entire unit could be constructed of different thicknesses and colors of plexiglass.

B. Altman and Company, Macy's and Bloomingdale's have all launched expanded operations for edibles, utensils and food service. The Altman ads in particular are quite smartly illustrated.

Cheese is becoming a very hot specialty food in this country. Shops can be designed to resemble a cheese box with a simple overhead interlocking frame from which cheeses can be hung. Switzerland, with its genuine cheeses represented here in the States by their own association, has provided promotional photos and materials to be used in merchandising their products.

In the meat group, a series of illustrations designed specifically for newspapers shows how technique can be controlled for reproduction. Clean, sharp lines, few solid areas, bold type, and borders complete the campaign.

The number of shops, boutiques and entire stores devoted to the sale of cooking equipment and foods has increased rapidly in the last ten years. Some innovators are Chuck Williams, President of Williams-Sonoma, with their beautiful stores, and the Crate and Barrel organization in Chicago, with their award-winning interiors.

With multi-million dollar volumes possible in gourmet merchandising (provided there is strict adherence to quality design), a great deal of money can be made in this field. Current outlets are a far cry from the utilitarian hardware stores and housewares departments of the past. The Crate and Barrel stores continue their tradition of tasteful display that has characterized this chain since its origin on Wells Street in Old Town of Chicago. The walls, columns, ceilings and casework are sheathed in pine; floors are white oak on upper levels of the store. The interiors, merchandisers, counters and displays are neutral in feeling, allowing the products to be seen and to dominate any area.

As indicated from the decor direction taken by Crate and Barrel, trends point to a natural look with black lettering. Other merchandise islands are painted in soft beige, and color accents range from tan and carmel to tuscan red. Merchandisers can be made in the shape of various cooking and food symbols, including a chicken with an egg-shaped shelf and hanging utensils.

Kitchen Crafts is a four-sided free-standing unit using simple graphics, indirect lighting and staggered display shelves. It can be constructed with any of the well-known fixture systems (Kasson, Abstracta) or produced "in-shop" with tubular steel or pine framing. Many of the ideas featured in this section can be used for displays. Designs can be cut out and mounted to panels or silkscreened directly to the panels.

BERRY PATCH

T BAGGS

TEAS OF ALLSORTS

domestic imported

Tea

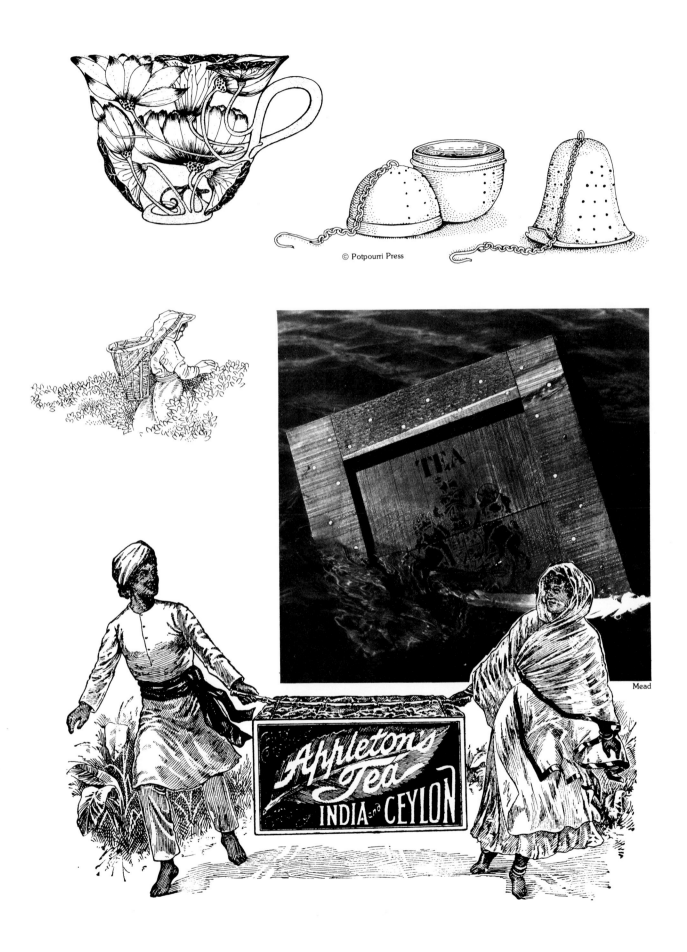

© Potpourri Press

Mead

Appleton's Tea
INDIA and CEYLON

Coffee

SANTOS

FRENCH ROAST

JAMAICAN BLUE MOUNTAIN

COLOMBIAN

MEXICAN

JAVA

MOCHA

98

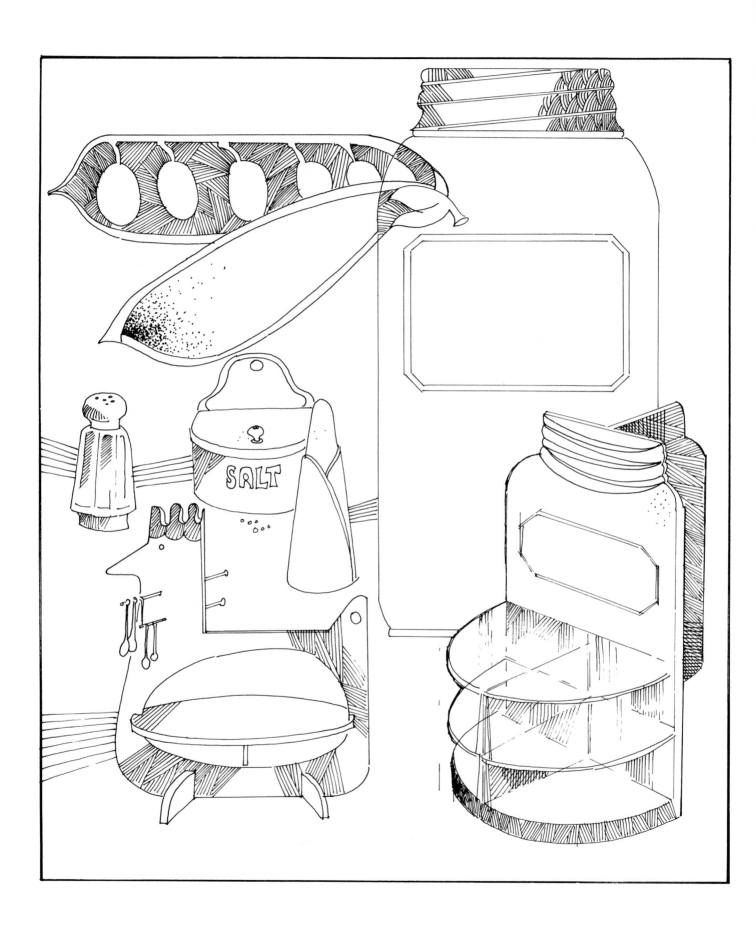

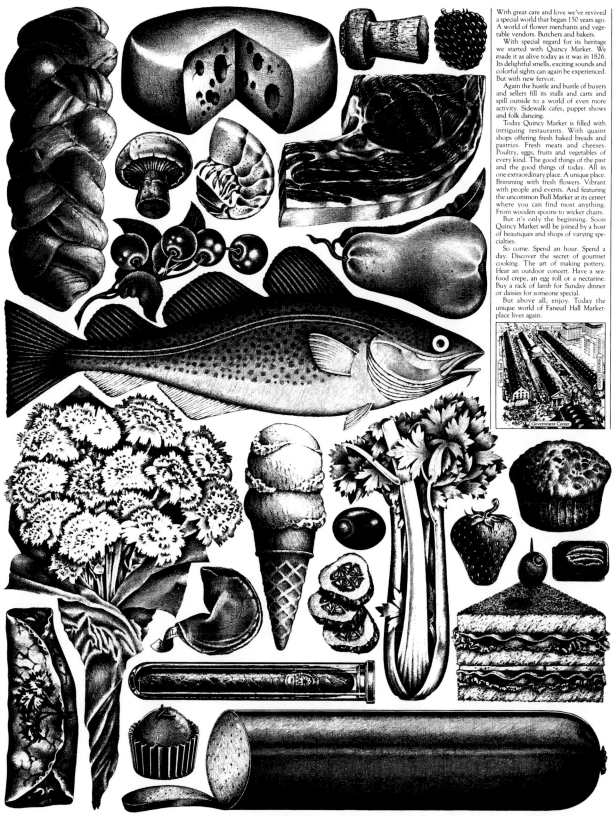

With great care and love we've revived a special world that began 150 years ago. A world of flower merchants and vegetable vendors. Butchers and bakers.

With special regard for its heritage we started with Quincy Market. We made it as alive today as it was in 1826. Its delightful smells, exciting sounds and colorful sights can again be experienced. But with new fervor.

Again the hustle and bustle of buyers and sellers fill its stalls and carts and spill outside to a world of even more activity. Sidewalk cafes, puppet shows and folk dancing.

Today Quincy Market is filled with intriguing restaurants. With quaint shops offering fresh baked breads and pastries. Fresh meats and cheeses. Poultry, eggs, fruits and vegetables of every kind. The good things of the past and the good things of today. All in one extraordinary place. A unique place. Brimming with fresh flowers. Vibrant with people and events. And featuring the uncommon Bull Market at its center where you can find most anything. From wooden spoons to wicker chairs.

But it's only the beginning. Soon Quincy Market will be joined by a host of beautiques and shops of varying specialties.

So come. Spend an hour. Spend a day. Discover the secret of gourmet cooking. The art of making pottery. Hear an outdoor concert. Have a seafood crepe, an egg roll or a nectarine. Buy a rack of lamb for Sunday dinner or daisies for someone special.

But above all, enjoy. Today the unique world of Faneuil Hall Marketplace lives again.

Today Faneuil Hall Marketplace is making history. Again.

B. Altman & Co

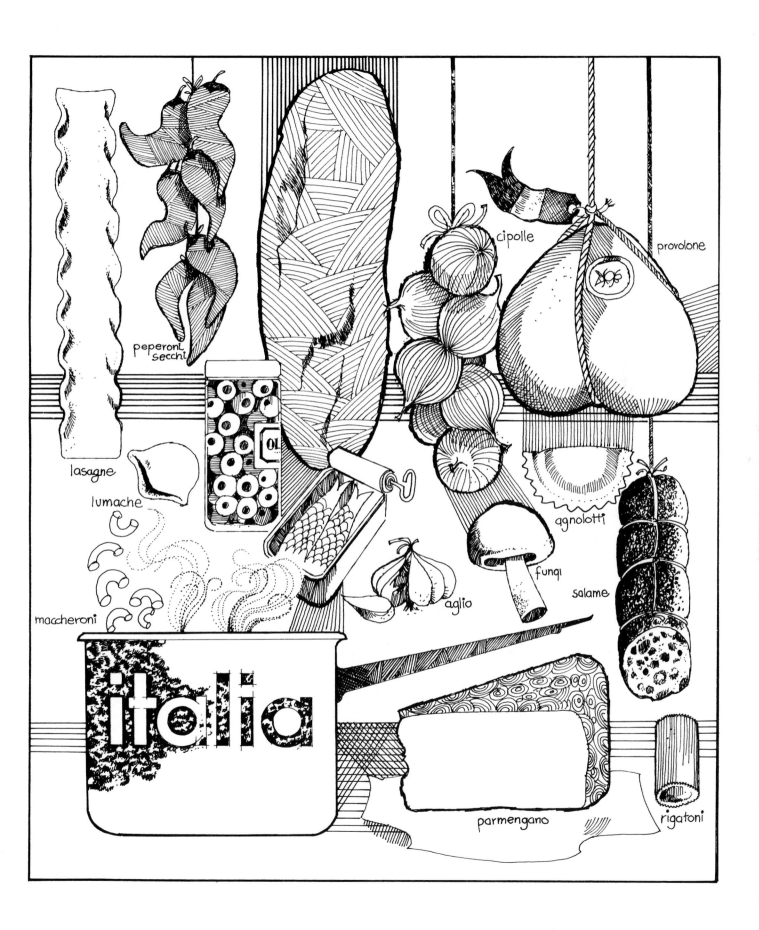

peperoni
secchi

cipolle

provolone

lasagne

lumache

OL

agnolotti

funqi

salame

maccheroni

aglio

italia

parmengano

rigatoni

103

© Dairy Bureau of Canada © Norseland Foods Inc.

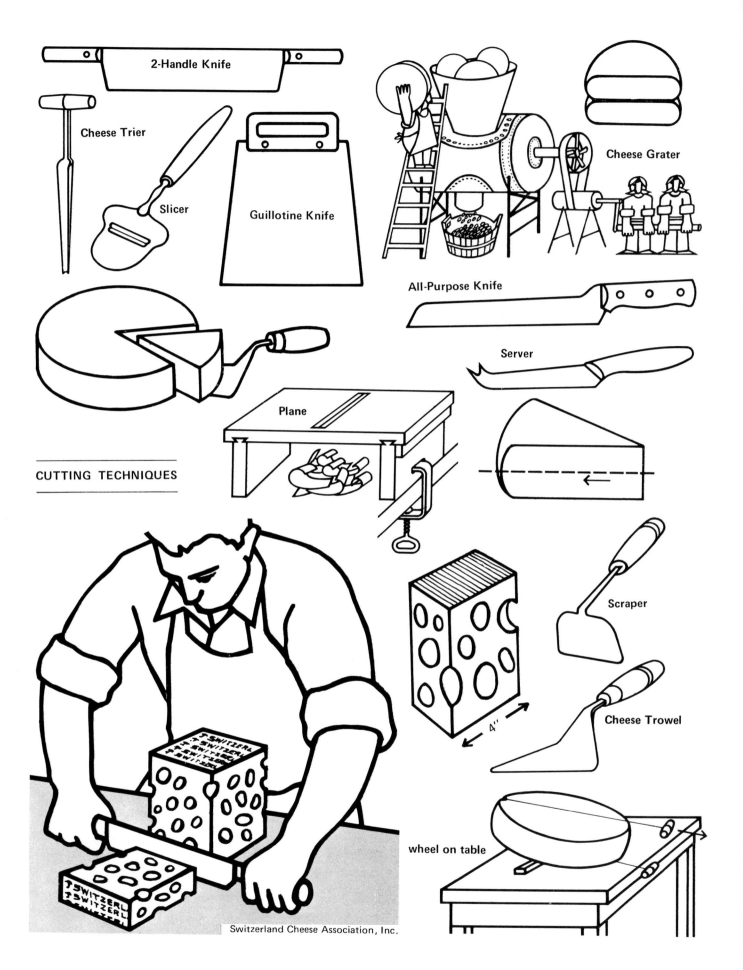

2-Handle Knife

Cheese Trier

Slicer

Guillotine Knife

Cheese Grater

All-Purpose Knife

Server

Plane

CUTTING TECHNIQUES

Scraper

4"

Cheese Trowel

wheel on table

Switzerland Cheese Association, Inc.

106

Pork Patties

Polynesian Pork

Danish Style Pork

Stir-Fry Pork
and Vegetables

Porkabob

Apple Glazed Ham

© Ontario Pork Producers Board

BEEF BARN

BŒUF

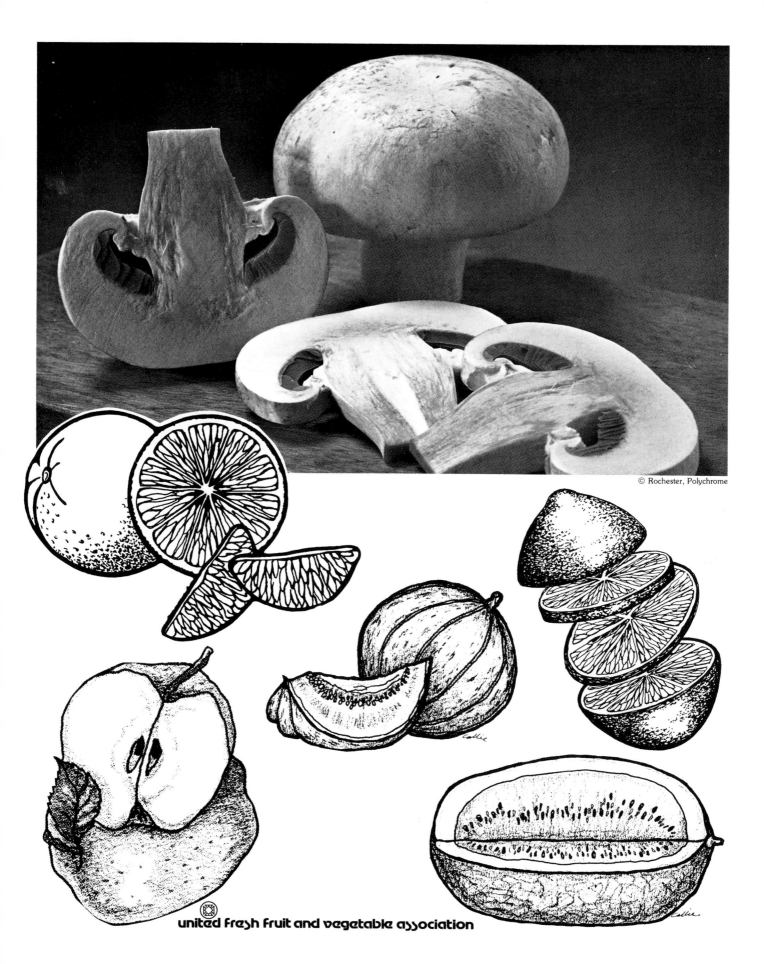

© Rochester, Polychrome

united fresh fruit and vegetable association

110

united fresh fruit and vegetable association

© Rochester, Polychrome

FRANCE

Chateau, the classic French castle or manor house, is a perfect symbol to open this section. The most beautiful ones were built in the central and southern areas during the period from the 12th to 15th centuries.

The word "chateau" generally means the county seat of a feudal lord or noble landowner. In the middle ages they were fortresses with central towers — donjons (dungeons) and water-filled moats. Improved living conditions led to the chateau de plaisance, "pleasure palace".

Using the arch and donjon shapes, a chateau has been designed for a boutique within a retail store. Carts, tiles and pedestals are the central motifs.

From the majestic chateau to a small and warm French country house, we find another area for merchandising and promotion. Here the French provincial countryside is dotted with charming farm villages and, as the traveler moves south, he will come upon those thatched roofs of the region called Camarque.

COM^E JOIN THE NEW DUNGE^ON

New Salad Bar ❧ Fantastic Wine Cocktails ❧ All New Menus ❧ Lunch ❧ Dinner ❧ Snacks ❧ Happy Hour: Monday through Friday 4 to 6 p.m. Free Popcorn ❧ Game Room ❧ Big Screen TV ❧ 1110 N.E. 2nd St. Corvallis · 503· 752·6903

the Dungeon
Pub & Grub

Don Weller

the Dungeon

the chateau

Schielda

©Folkwear 1975

FRENCH CHEESEMAKER'S SMOCK

chateux
market

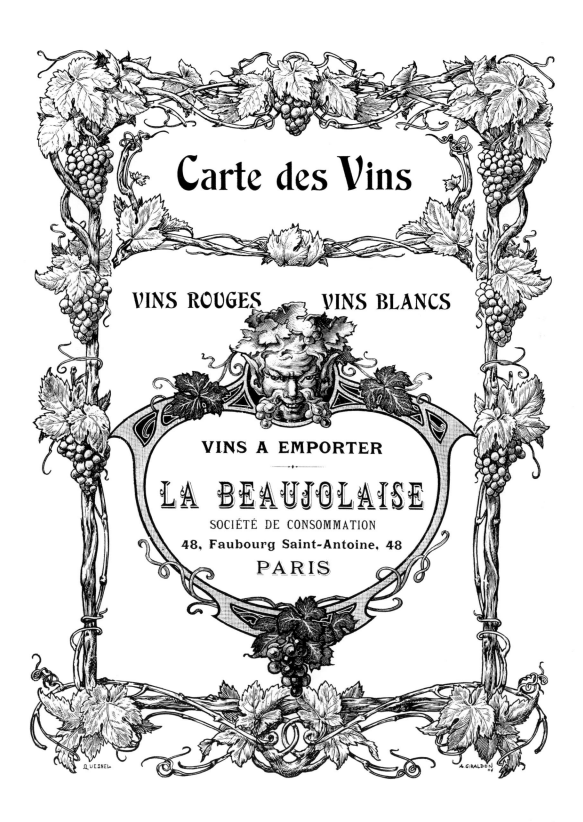

Carte des Vins

VINS ROUGES   VINS BLANCS

VINS A EMPORTER

LA BEAUJOLAISE

SOCIÉTÉ DE CONSOMMATION

48, Faubourg Saint-Antoine, 48

PARIS

QUESNEL   A. GIRALDON

© Dynamic Graphics

GREECE

Vasilion tis Ellados — the kingdom of Hellas. This jewel in the Mediterranean is a country of seafarers. No part of Greece is more than 85 miles from the sea.

Promotions and merchandising usually show euzone — the colorful palace guards. On these pages are additional ideas — vases, amphora, column sections, a country cart and the famous windmills along the sea.

BBARBER.

OLYMPIC
AIRWAYS
THE AIRLINE TO THE CLASSICAL WORLD

© Olympic Airways

Holland remains a European show-case with its startling contrasts — overpowering with its wonders. A land pitted against the sea, its lush green meadows are laced with placid inland waterways. Colorful canal boats ply the locks; and suddenly, you are within the environs of one of its seven major cities - Amsterdam, Rotterdam, The Hague, Utrecht, Groningen, Breda and Eidhoven.

The symbols are countless: unique lift bridges over the canals against a backdrop of 16th and 17th century houses, three hundred year old windmills like the "Barremolen" in Zoeterwoude and the graceful sailing barges on the Zuiderzee.

For centuries, Alkmaar, 25 miles north of Amsterdam has been "cheese town." Here, auctions are held that draw hundreds of spectators every Friday from early May through September. The now famous Waagebouw (Weigh House) was originally a chapel that became a meat market in 1578, and later a renaissance facade was added and a clock tower. Today, the dealers are in the dockside Weigh House by 9 in the morning when the first barges pull up. The dock teams move the cheeses from the quay to the Weigh House and the dealers wait to bid on them.

Red, yellow, blue and green straw hats denote the various guild teams and many of the workers, dressed in sparkling white uniforms, are descendants of 400 years of cheesemaking. They carry the famous hand barrows (stretchers with sides built up) decorated with pennants and streamers to match their hats. It's a picture that is duplicated nowhere else in the world — a colorful panorama of red and golden balls of cheese, pink houses, brightly colored hats and flags flying from the barges. The sun sparkling on the quiet waters of the canal and beyond a windmill turning lazily against a delft blue sky. There's so much more to this very famous country, including a visit to see the treasury of masterpieces in the Frans Hals museum in Haarlem.

HOLLANDAZE

B BARBER

126

© Province of Ontario Ministry of Tourism

EDAM

ALKMAAR

Freelance Photographers Guild

127

ICE CREAM PARLORS

At the turn of the century (before the days of dieting), the neighborhood ice cream parlor was a favorite gathering place. Men wore moustache protectors to keep their handlebars clean. The setting was pure joy — grey marble counters and soda tables, rich mahogany cabinets, bentwood or metal chairs, and beautiful Tiffany lamps with the Coca-Cola or Moxie names right in the shade.

Interest in the "good ol' days" has brought about recycled and restored fountains of yesteryear. The Ghirardelli Chocolate Manufactory and Soda Fountain is a highlight of the building complex in San Francisco (see Malls and Markets). Other stores, like Serendipity in New York and Marshal Fields Crystal Parlor are famous for their ice cream concoctions.

Others confections lend themselves to promotions similar to those used by NBC with their Candy Bar Cookalikes. Letraset uses the traditional forms, such as M & M's, Lifesavers, and cookies, to promote their line of pressure sensitive products.

© Coca Cola Co.

© NBC/WMAQ

Hank Aaron: Babe Ruth's Successor.
Tonight at 6:30 on WMAQ-TV, Irv Kupcinet interviews the man who speaks softly and carries a big stick.

© George Stavrinos

Illustrators

For every page by the many illustrators represented in this section, one will find a variety of styles and techniques. Some of the illustrators are well known, others less so. For the unknowns, exposure will no doubt increase with this book. Background material has been provided for a few illustrators who have made this information available.

ROBERT SCHNEEBERG

Robert Schneeberg was born in 1922 in Philadelphia, where he was raised and schooled. He is a graduate of the highly respected Philadelphia College of Art. His work has appeared in Mademoiselle, Good Housekeeping and Cosmopolitan.

He began designing for Hallmark Cards in 1954 and joined the firm on an exclusive basis in 1965. He was commissioned to design four murals for the new Crown Center Hotel's Coffee Garden. Two are wooden collages, one is ceramic, and one is metal.

Schneeberg says his art training began when he started copying the funny papers as a child, and today he doesn't presume to call himself an artist. He says he's a "decorative illustrator."

Schneeberg is best known for his murals and "American Primitive" collages. His work has been called everything from "outstanding . . . native American folk art" to "primitive as children's art and just as charming." His effect is achieved through the marriage of primitive folk art styles with contemporary collage techniques.

Schneeberg, his wife, Ann, and their daughter, Ann Elizabeth, live in Bucks County, Pennsylvania. Weekends, the family enjoys lazy drives through Pennsylvania Dutch country, a rich source of ideas for Schneeberg.

For diversion, Schneeberg builds rock walls, brick paths and scratches around in a backyard garden, planted with ferns, woods, stumps and rocks — but no flowers. He gets inspiration there, and from early American handmade toys, from history books, craft collections and historical sites.

Picasso, innovator of the collage technique, is among Schneeberg's favorite artists. "For any contemporary artist not to respect Picasso and be tremendously influenced by him would be very difficult to understand."

Though Robert Schneeberg may not call himself an artist, we can see the outstanding murals in the lobby level Coffee Garden and decide for ourselves.

ALAIN MOREAU

A native of France, Alain Moreau came to the United States in 1964. He earned his fine arts degree in Grenoble, graduating with honors. After moving to Los Angeles, he attended The Art Center College of Design and began his career as a graphic designer and freelance illustrator. He soon established himself as a reputable artist and subsequently, has worked for the Los Angeles Civic Light Opera, painted album covers for Angel, ABC, Paramount and Warner records. He also made countless contributions to N.F.L. publications.

Moreau's work has received numerous awards from the Los Angeles Art Directors Club and the prestigious New York Society of Illustrators. In the 1976 Bicentennial, his painting titled "World's First One-Hour Flight" was selected for the Air Force Bicentennial Exhibition at the Pentagon in Washington,

GEORGE S. GAADT

George S. Gaadt at 30 is one of the new generation of illustrators whose creativity in line and form, and bold and imaginative use of color has caught the eye of the serious critic and won him a place in significant exhibitions and shows across the country.

George Gaadt was born in Erie, Pennsylvania, in 1941. He was graduated from Columbus College of Art & Design, Columbus, Ohio, where, during his undergraduate years, he worked in advertising. His experience in illustrating has included periods of design work for national companies in Cleveland, Columbus, and Kansas City.

Recognition came early for Mr. Gaadt. While still in school he won a Merit Award from the New York Society of Illustrators College Scholarship Contest. Since then he has exhibited in a number of shows where he also took honors for his work. In the past four years his paintings, singly and in portfolio, have been included in the New York Society of Illustrators show, Pittsburgh's ACE show, and the National Educational Television show in Miami. There he was awarded a Gold Medal for book design, and illustrating a television series, "Because We Care."

DON WELLER

Don Weller is a graphic designer/illustrator/filmmaker/photographer. His formal education ended with a BA degree from Washington State University in 1960. He worked for 6 years at various design studios and freelanced illustration, then opened his own studio in 1966 and began teaching graphic design at ULCA. He incorporated with Dennis Juett (Weller & Juett) in 1970, and formed The Weller Institute for the Cure of Design in 1973 where he works at present in the capacity of "founder." He also teaches design and illustration at Art Center College of Design.

Clients of the Weller Institute come from most major cities in the United States and Tokyo. In 1976 he married Chikako Matsubayashi who has held the position of the Weller Institute "design doctor" since 1973. They live with a dog and a cat in the institute offices in Bridgewater, Connecticut and/or Los Angeles.

Weller is past president of the Los Angeles Society of Illustrators. His work has been exhibited in nearly all of the major national (USA) and international graphic design exhibitions and magazines including Graphis, Photographis, Typomundus 20/2, American Institute of Graphic Arts, Communication Arts, The Art Directors Club of New York Exhibition (including gold medals and silver medals), New York Illustrators Exhibit, Illustration West, Creativity on Paper Show (New York), The New York Type Directors Club Suite 16 Exhibition, Paper Power (Mead Library of Ideas), Creativity (New York), and others.

NORMAN BAXTER

Norman Baxter has a varied art background. He spent four years as a layout artist for a retail store, and five years as a freelance artist. In 1957, he co-founded Baxter and Korge, Inc., a communications design firm. In 1961, he sold his interest in the firm but continued as an illustrator. He returned to freelance art in 1977.

For three years, Baxter has done the Southwestern Bell Yellow Pages for St. Louis, Kansas City, Dallas, and Houston. He has done watercolor series of ten scenes each for Texas, Florida, Tennessee, and the West for DeLuxe Check Printers. He has also produced work for Houston Natural Gas and Texaco. He has also published a hardbound book of 160 pen and ink drawings called "A Line on Texas," which came out in softbound in 1980.

Some of the awards Norman Baxter has received are from New York Art Directors Club, Dallas-Fort Worth Art Directors Club, Art Direction, and Grand Prix, Houston. He now devotes his time to pen and ink or watercolors at his Houston studio.

HILLAIR HENRIE ROBINSON

Hillair Henrie Robinson is a gypsy at heart, and has traveled throughout Europe and the U.S., filling many sketchbooks with her drawings and observations. It was one of these sketchbooks that won her a guest editorship with Mademoiselle magazine in 1976. She has freelanced in New York, Boston, San Francisco, Salt Lake City and Graz, Austria, and spent time in Finland doing sketches and research for a children's book.

Hillair found enough time in between her peregrinations to attend Utah State University where she graduated in 1978, when she was awarded the "Talent of the Year" award for her outstanding achievements in the arts.

Hillair's work has been published in Communication Arts, Mademoiselle and the Los Angeles Illustrators Annual. She is currently working as a designer/illustrator for Salt Lake's largest design studio, L.D.S. Graphics, where she is involved in designing educational and other material for use in 58 countries worldwide.

Hillair Henrie Robinson

134

The Printing Paper Division of Weyerhaeuser in Plymouth Meeting, Pennsylvania is constantly producing excellent pieces of high quality promotional work. Their "Innovations in Paper" series devoted to the tales of the Orient Express is no exception. This famous train traveled 1900 miles from Paris to Constantinople in three nights and two days. It was the train of kings and couriers, of diplomats and businessmen, of lovers and smugglers and just plain people who wanted to travel with maximum comfort in minimum fuss. It was too, the scene of many thrilling books by Agatha Christie, Graham Greene and Ian Fleming to name a few.

Jackie Miles produced the watercolor illustration of the chef and woman, William Goldberg illustrated King Boris, Linda and John Gist produced the Harem scene, and Vince Cucinotta illustrated the German prisoners. Grey and Rogers of Philadelphia was the agency.

Koh-I-Noor

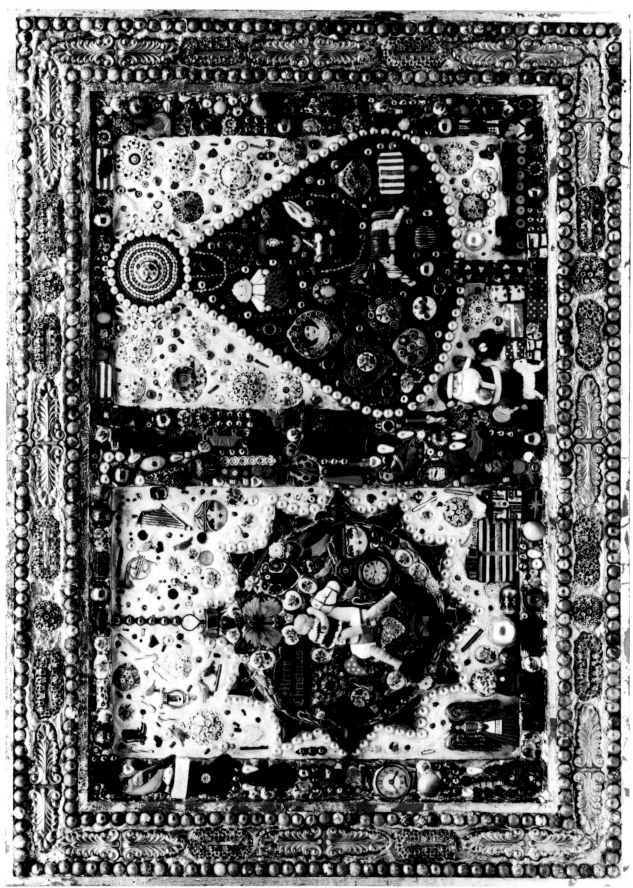

Robert Schneeberg for Hallmark

136

French Halberd 1750

Montcalm

Colours of the La Reine Regiment

French Officer 1750's

The French were closely allied with many of the Great Lakes Indians.

French Grenadier Officers 1757 saluting and carrying a Fusil in regulation position

Plate IV.

© George Gaadt

137

Weyerhaeuser artist Vince Cucinotta

140

Pitt Studios artist L. Taylor

Don Weller

142

Alain Moreau

143

Weyerhaeuser artists Linda and John Gist

144

Keith McConnell

Pendleton.
The All-American tradition of quality sportswear for four generations.

FOR FURTHER INFORMATION, WRITE DEPT. XN, PENDLETON WOOLEN MILLS, PORTLAND, OREGON 97201

147

Dave Mariani

Airport Marina Hotel artist Jack Unruh

149

Pierce Arrow

Ken Dallison

"The Infamy of Toad-stool" was a favorite headline used by Pierce-Arrow. The headline would be justified on the 1929 Model 133 dual cowl phaeton, top. It was the same year they introduced the straight eights with the X head, giving 125 h.p. Above right is the 1930 Model B rumble-seat roadster. Left the 1931 Club Brougham.

© George Stavrinos

151

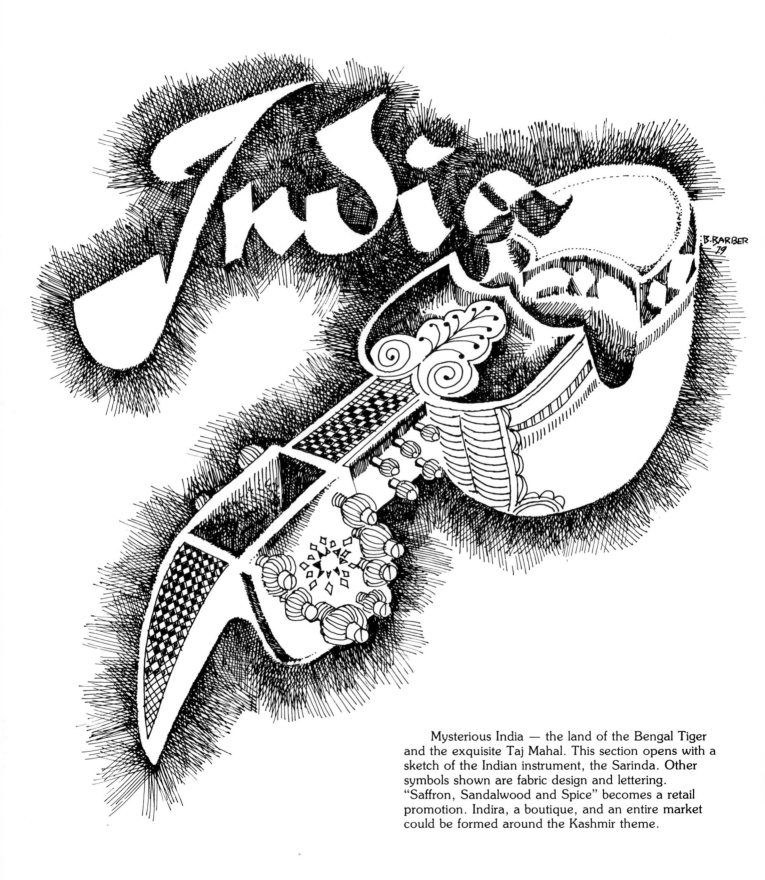

Mysterious India — the land of the Bengal Tiger and the exquisite Taj Mahal. This section opens with a sketch of the Indian instrument, the Sarinda. Other symbols shown are fabric design and lettering. "Saffron, Sandalwood and Spice" becomes a retail promotion. Indira, a boutique, and an entire market could be formed around the Kashmir theme.

© Potpourri Press

153

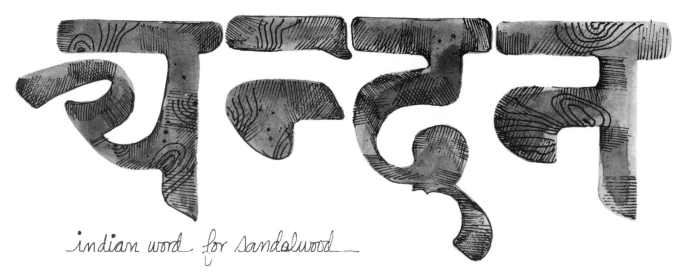

indian word for sandalwood

IRELAND

Ireland has been described as the home of friendliness, a kaleidoscope of the past and present. George Bernard Shaw might have put it best when he said, "Ireland, Sir, for good or evil is like no other place under Heaven".

These pages are devoted to a few glimpses of the architecture of this famous island — the thatched farm houses in the highlands of Donagal and some factory row houses from one of its cities. Also included are a few Vince Cucinottas line drawings from the fascinating Weyerhauser paper promotion on golf in Ireland.

The potential for promotions and graphics of Dublin's pubs alone is tremendous. Longhall, that friendliest of pubs is filled with huge collections of antiques. In James Joyce's book "Ulysses", his character, Mr. Bloom stopped at Davey Burnes for a glass of burgundy and a piece of Gorgonzola. Other Irish symbols are the traditional jaunting cart and gypsy wagon. And those famous names that trip on the tongue — Derry, Bellina, Carrickmacross, Balbriggan, Tralee, Skibbereen, Lisdoonvarna, Crossmolina and Graiguenamanagh . . . Whew!

You'll find the Irish tourists boards in New York, Chicago, San Francisco and Toronto along with the Irish international airlines, Aerlingus to be most helpful.

Castelmaine milk wagon

Weyerhaeuser artist Vince Cucinotta

155

Weyerhaeuser artist Vince Cucinotta

156

Wednesday at Kinsale

the ISLANDS

They dot the oceans all over the world. The Bahamas claims Harbour Island off Florida as one of the jewels in its string. This is a wonderful spot — rich with lore about Spanish Galleons sailing among the islands to avoid bad weather during the plunder of the Incas. These islands are well-known today for scuba diving — Gingerbread grounds, Spanish wells, Turtle Rocks, and the Luford Cay dropoff.

The Pacific Area Travel Association, with its montage of symbols, reminds us of the vast region that comprises the Pacific — from Thailand and Australia all the way north to Japan, east to Alaska, Canada and the states, and south to Galapagos and the Fijis.

On Oahu's north shore, the Polynesian Cultural Center has established a unique place where guests can explore the charm and beauty of seven South Pacific islands in one day — Marquesas, Hawaii, Tahiti, Fiji, New Zealand, Samoa, and Tonga. Canoe tours and train rides are offered along with crafts and native foods. It is certianly worth a trip.

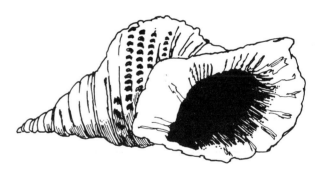

Polynesian Cultural Center

United Airlines

© Livingstone Evans

160

Polynesian Cultural Center

ROSA MARIA

© Nick Galloway

Pacific Area Travel Assn.

163

pacific

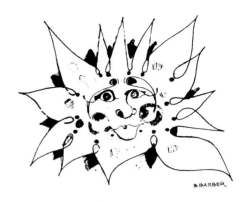

B BARBER

HARBOUR ISLAND

165

ITALIA

This section opens with a carbineer's hat. The pages are devoted to the southern half of the country — Pisa, Venice, and Rome. Like the German beer steins, the famed Chianti bottle almost serves as a symbol of Italy.

Freelance Photographers Guild

Alitalia

© Dynamic Graphics

168

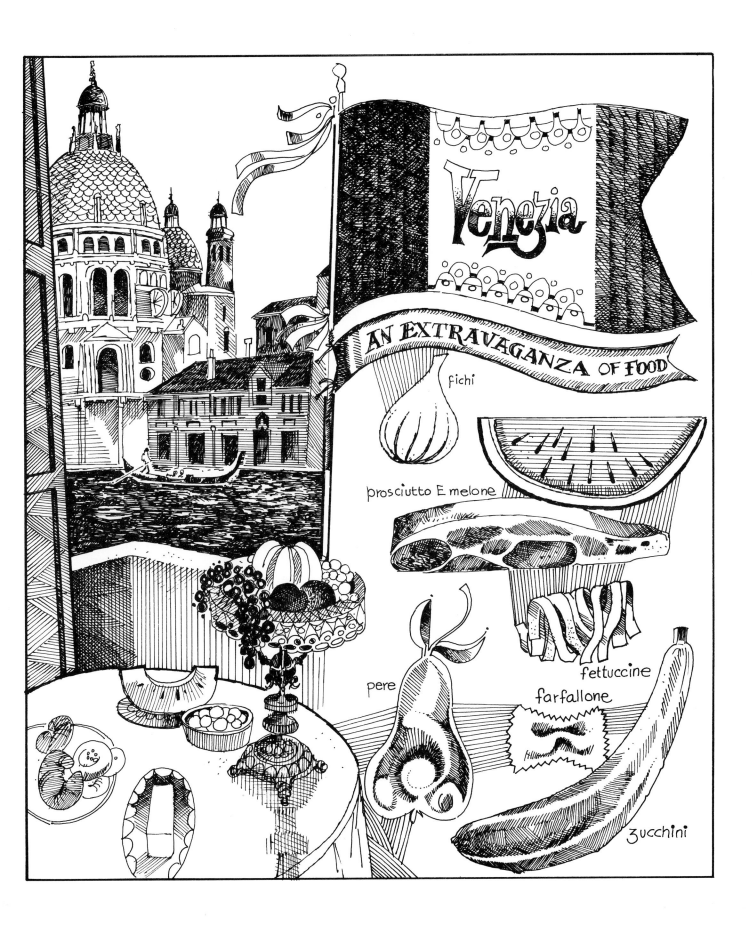

Venezia

AN EXTRAVAGANZA OF FOOD

fichi

prosciutto E melone

pere

fettuccine

farfallone

zucchini

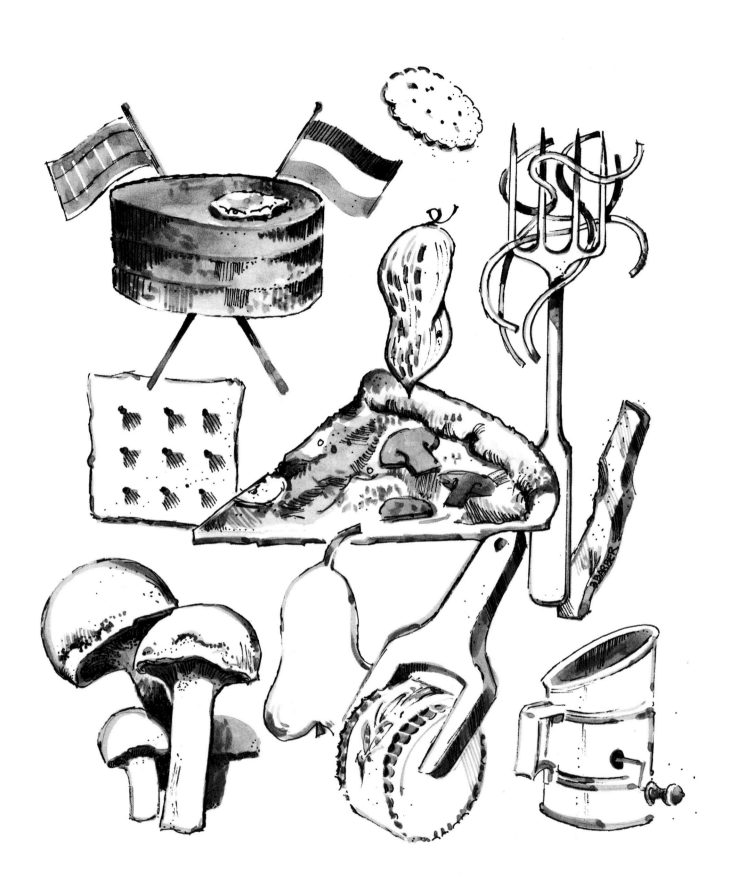

ROMA

Leonardos

B. BARBER

172

THE LEGENDARY CONESTOGA

The Conestoga was a rugged wagon used by the American pioneers in their move west. Both ends were built higher than the middle (the better to cross rivers with) and the wheels were complete with broad rims to prevent bogging down in mud. Drawn by four or six horses, they were called "camels of the prairies."

In this day and age, a wheeled wagon handmade of wood and iron, moving along smoothly on its darkly greased axles, is a sight we seldom if ever see unless we have the good fortune to be in the deep countryside where a few of these wonderful vehicles are still used. England and other countries on the continent have great groups of native gypsies who still travel in their elaborately decorated wagons.

Gypsy Wagon

ALA CARTE

ICES

PURE ICES

lancashire
icecream cart

CHUCK'S
WAGON

175

Malls and Markets

Ghirardelli Square

"The Market Movement" began with the old Ghirardelli Chocolate Factory in San Francisco. In 1962, Mrs. William P. Roth and her son, shipping magnate William Matson Roth, purchased a group of 19th century red brick buildings, capped by a clock tower that perched on the hill at 900 North Point. Its warehouse was named after Domenico Ghirardelli, founder of the chocolate dynasty that had occupied the site since 1892.

After Roth purchased the entire block, he formed an action group and started looking for a development concept. He settled on Lawrence Halpirn, Wurster Bernardi and Emmons, John Matthias and others. The final result of their work is now "a beehive of excitement," in the words of Larry Halpirn.

"Gear-ar-delly" is a multi-sensory delight — laughter, flowers, music, Turkish bread, a wine cellar, people taking pictures of people taking pictures, Japanese food, views of San Francisco hills and the beautiful Bay, a sensuous bronze and copper mermaid fountain, beer gardens, sirloin steaks, super hot fudge sundaes, and a beautiful girl playing beautiful music in the center of the Plaza. In essence, a huge, bright and happy bazaar.

Ghirardelli was the first in an amazing series of shopping center renovations and reconstructions that dot the United States. In its home town of San Francisco, it was followed by the Cannery, then (not necessarily in chronological order) Trolley Square in Salt Lake City, Faneuil Hall Marketplace in Boston, Larimer Square in Denver, and Factor's Walk in Savannah, to name a few.

After these early pioneering efforts came the more modern concepts, such as Citicorp Center in New York, Embarcadero Center in San Francisco, and Water Tower Place in Chicago. Some new "old" places are Olla Podrida in Dallas, New Market in Philadelphia, Freight House Square in Pittsburgh, Pier 39 in San Francisco, and Harbor Place in Baltimore, the most recent Rouse Company development.

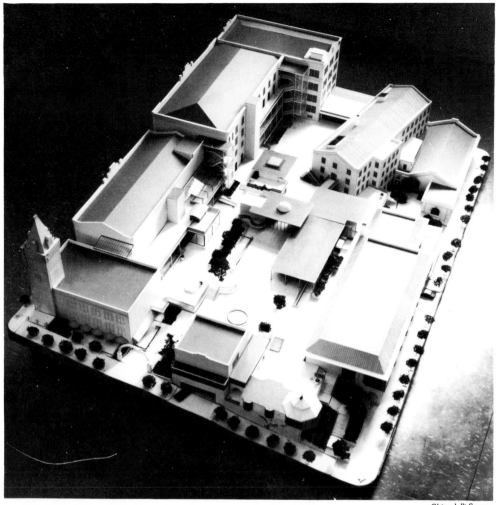

Ghirardelli Square

Faneuil Hall Marketplace

Faneuil Hall Marketplace was redeveloped into a contemporary urban commercial center in the heart of downtown Boston. Adjacent to Faneuil Hall, the Marketplace consists of three long parallel buildings: Quincy Market, North and South Market buildings and the streets between. The Market complex was developed by Mayor Josiah Quincy in 1826 as an extension of Faneuil Hall, Boston's first public food market. The three buildings designed in the Greek Revival Style by architect Alexander Parris, were built on filled land once used as the town dock. Because the project was initiated by city government using reclaimed land, the Markets project of 1826 is often referred to as America's first example of urban renewal. The Markets, considered the architectural pride of Boston, remained in continuous operation, but fell into disrepair and neglect in the late 1950's.

The redevelopment of the Market complex began in 1964 as part of the Boston Redevelopment Authority's Waterfront Urban Renewal project. With city renewal funds and a $2 million HUD grant, the BRA acquired the buildings, relocated the food wholesalers, installed new utilities throughout the six-acre area, and restored the exterior facades.

In 1973 The Rouse Company of Columbia, Maryland, was designated by the BRA as developer of the Markets. The Rouse Company with the architectural firm of Benjamin Thompson and Associates, Cambridge, Massachusetts, created and executed a plan to revitalize Mayor Quincy's legacy. After Jim Rouse worked out his problems with the New York and Boston Banks, the Quincy Market had its grand opening on August 26, 1976.

A principal part of the Quincy Market is the Bull Market. Located in the rotunda and under the glass canopies, the Bull Market has been named after the bull weathervane atop the building's copper dome. It consists of a variety of merchants and artisans selling unusual wares, ranging from pickles to pots, in small carts and stands.

The flanking South and North Market buildings re-opened in 1977. The three lower levels of each building feature a variety of distinctive shops, including apparel and accessories for men and women, crafts and imports, home furnishings, art galleries, sporting goods, and more restaurants with night-time activities. The three upper levels were divided into individual offices.

177

The streets separating the three buildings are now closed to vehicular traffic. Landscaped and paved with brick, cobblestone, and granite, the streets provide space for merchandise stands, artists, craftsmen, and changing promotional activities. South Market Street is the connecting link to Boston's "Walkway to the Sea" that begins at Government Center and terminates at the new 4-1/2 acre Waterfront Park.

The now famous Faneuil Hall Marketplace in Boston is a phenomenon that attracts over 10 million visitors a year, surpassing Disneyland in attendance. It has the essential ingredient that Rouse calls "a spirit of festival." Like Ghirardelli Square, Faneuil Hall is a mix of good taste and great design, which make shopping fun.

Today, this marketing complex stands as a tribute to its developer, James W. Rouse. He is by far the leading expert in revitalizing innercity retailing. His projects are attractive and invite an intermingling of activities — shopping, eating, and best of all, people watching. Rouse has social awareness and a deep commitment to making cities better places to live and work.

PIER 39

In 1974 the Port Commission of San Francisco invited bids for private commercial development of the waterfront in San Francisco from Pier 9 to 24. Warren Simmons, a native San Franciscan, ex-Pan Am pilot, restauranteur and real estate developer, submitted his plan with his architects, Bruce Moody and David Walker. In March of 1975, his proposal was granted. Pier 39 is a gigantic development, costing over $54 million that today houses over 24 restaurants and 110 specialty shops.

The 45 acre site is a quarter of a mile long, 180 feet at the shore and 350 feet at the Bay end, with marinas flanking both sides. The once abandoned cargo pier has been transformed into the largest single development built on San Francisco's northern waterfront since 1940 and ranks with Disneyworld as one of the major tourist attractions in the country.

To create an authentic maritime atmosphere, one third of the structures, as well as the first and second level walkways are built of aged, weathered wood salvaged from the demolished structures of several of the original piers. The restaurants offer the finest food to be found in San Francisco with every type of food imaginable, including Polynesian, French and the traditional San Francisco seafood.

For entertainment, strolling musicians, magicians, jugglers, famous San Francisco street artists, Pier 39's own rainmaker and a world renowned high diving team perform regularly at the three staging areas located throughout the complex. In addition to these entertainments, the Pier presents a year round celebration of San Francisco, with special events including lighted boat parades, wind surfing exhibitions, kite flying contests, a waterfront Christmas fair and more.

Faneuil Hall Marketplace

178

HARBORPLACE

Harborplace consists of two glass-enclosed pavilions overlooking Baltimore's Inner Harbor. The Light Street Pavilion, on the western shore, features restaurants and cafes, market and specialty foods, and a wide variety of small eating places. The Pratt Street Pavilion, on the northern edge of the Harbor, houses small specialty shops and restaurants and cafes with harbor views.

Harborplace, at the corner of Pratt and Light Streets, is located at the heart of Baltimore's revitalized financial and office district, within easy walking distance of the new Convention Center, the Maryland Science Center, and the National Aquarium in Baltimore, scheduled to open soon. Overhead pedestrian walkways will link the Light Street Pavilion to the Hyatt Regency Hotel and from there to the Central Business District.

The two pavilions occupy a site which has a combined land area of 3.12 acres. Both buildings are 40 feet high and have two levels. The Light Street Pavilion is 420 feet long and 220 feet wide. The Pratt Street Pavilion is 450 feet long and 104 feet wide. Total gross leasable area is 142,000 square feet.

The merchant/tenants occupying Harborplace are approximately 150 businesses, primarily local and owner-operated, reflecting the character and life styles of Baltimore and the Chesapeake Bay region.

The developer was Harborplace Limited Partnership, a subsidiary of The Rouse Company and the architect was Benjamin Thompson & Associates of Cambridge, Massachusetts, the same firm that collaborated with The Rouse Company on The Faneuil Hall Marketplace in Boston.

Harborplace will include more than 120 restaurants, sidewalk cafes, small eating places, market foods, and small specialty shops in two glass-enclosed pavilions. Each two-story pavilion, located on the edge of the Inner Harbor, has views of the harbor and the city, and access to hotels, the Convention Center, the Aquarium, and major downtown offices. Harborplace will be a year-round gathering place for shopping, eating and entertainment.

The Light Street Pavilion includes at ground level a Colonnade Market featuring purveyors of produce, fish, meat, and dairy foods, and a two-story skylit Trading Hall for wines, baked goods, gourmet foods and tobacco. On the second level a Food Hall, designed as an indoor park, will offer a variety of small eating places serving international foods. The adjoining Sam Smith Market, named for a Revolutionary war hero and former mayor, will be a colorful bazaar for a changing array of crafts and gift items.

The Pratt Street Pavilion has two levels of small specialty shops offering merchandise such as apparel, sporting goods, housewares and gifts. The shops, arranged along colonnades, are skylit on the second level. In both pavilions, restaurants and cafes with harborside terraces offer views of the harbor.

THE MARKET AT CITICORP CENTER

This magnificent market is at the base of the spectacular Hugh Stubbins & Associates Citicorp building, that has been termed one of the new generation of sky scrapers. The building is 59 stories, supported on four 24 feet square columns, each rising 120 feet high. A central core carries interior loads and the tower framing utilizes chevron bracing, carrying the tower loads to sound rock fifty feet below grade.

The Market at Citicorp Center is an international shopping and dining center, with the accent on food, food preparation and everything for the home and table. Culinary delights can be found in the form of a light snack to enjoy at a table in the skylit Atrium; a full-course lunch or dinner at one of the international restaurants; or a gourmet feast to take home. Shopping for home and table at The Market is a world tour, ranging from European housewares and home furnishings to imported chocolates, cookbooks of the world's great cuisines, fresh flowers, imported cigars, table linens, French bread and blended coffees and teas from around the globe.

The Market's restaurants feature food from many lands . . . including authentic specialties from Hungary, Italy, Greece, Switzerland, France, England and Scandinavia. Open 7 days a week, The Market is also the locale for a year-around program of free special events. The public is invited to enjoy a wide range of programs, from classical to jazz, while relaxing in the Atrium.

The Market occupies the first three levels of a seven-story low rise structure at the Citicorp Center complex. The complex, a development of Citibank, occupies most of the city block bordered by Lexington and Third Avenues and 53rd and 54th Streets. Those entering from the Lexington Avenue subway station or the Plaza at the corner of Lexington Avenue and 53rd Street can reach The Market by walking east through the arcade.

At the opposite corner, Third Avenue and 54th Street, one can enter Conran's, the first U.S. outlet of a well-known British home furnishings chain. The many entrances provide a natural pedestrian traffic flow to the center of the complex — The Market. In addition to the low rise structure, the Citicorp Center complex includes a 59-story tower building, a landscaped sunken plaza and the free-standing St. Peter's Church.

The Market occupants are varied and fascinating. Conran's occupies the largest amount of space, using

179

the entire upper level and a portion of the street level stores. Floral boutiques and book shops are also featured on the street level and over a dozen varied European town square type restaurants offer international food in great variety. Auberge Suisse, the Greek Avgerinos, Hungaria Restaurant designed and operated by the George Lang Corporation, Les Tournebroches, operated by the well-known restauranteur Charles Shevillot, Slotnick's Daughter, Healthworks and a magnificent display of Scandinavian specialties at Nyborg Nelson.

One of the most interesting and important parts of the development of Citicorp Center is St. Peter's Church. In 1969 the Lutheran congregation of St. Peter's Church voted to sell the property to First National City Bank and agreed to the demolition of the original church. In return, they received ownership of 45,000 sq. ft. of new church space on the same corner at 54th Street in Lexington.

Pastor of St. Peter's, Ralph E. Peterson, has been a moving force to guarantee that the spiritual needs of the congregation were met and he also wanted his church to be a hospice for anyone who wished to briefly join the church's activities. The exterior of the church is sharp, angular and somewhat cold, but inside all is warmth and richness. The chapel contains some magnificent Louise Nevelson sculptures, the pews are in rich wood, with needlepoint seats and the entire feeling is one of peace and tranquility. A true oasis on busy Lexington Avenue.

HARBORPLACE

FANEUIL HALL MARKETPLACE

Benjamin, Thompson and Assoc. Inc.

Today at 11:30 a.m. Faneuil Hall Marketplace becomes even more fun and even more exciting. Because starting today we'll not only be an intriguing world of food and flowers and fun, we'll be an enchanting world of fashion.

Starting today our South Market is ready. And it's delightful. We've kept its 151-year-old charm and warmth. You'll see it and feel it in the original brick and wood. We've added handsome contemporary touches to tastefully blend yesterday's world with today's. And we've filled it all with shops and stores full of beautiful things for you.

You'll find the newest fashions. In everything. From head to toe. From top to bottom. And jewelry, from the exotic to the primitive. We'll be just the place to find what's in for Fall and Spring and in between.

We'll be pinstripe suits and European pants. Buttondown collars and pullover sweaters. We'll be new hairstyles, your special scent of soap and favorite perfume. We'll be good books, unusual prints and fine furniture.

We'll be The Arcade. And The Gallery. Full of distinctive gifts from the world over. Elegant things for a home or for an office. Precious things for a friend or just for yourself.

But best of all, it will all be here. In one unique place. Full of fun. Full of beauty. Full of even more delicious foods. And now, full of the newest fashions. For everyone.

So come. Once again. Join the festivity. Buy a daisy. A pair of jeans. A spiffy scarf or the finest silky blouse.

But enjoy. Today Faneuil Hall Marketplace opens again. In style.

PIER 39

A Celebration of San Francisco

185

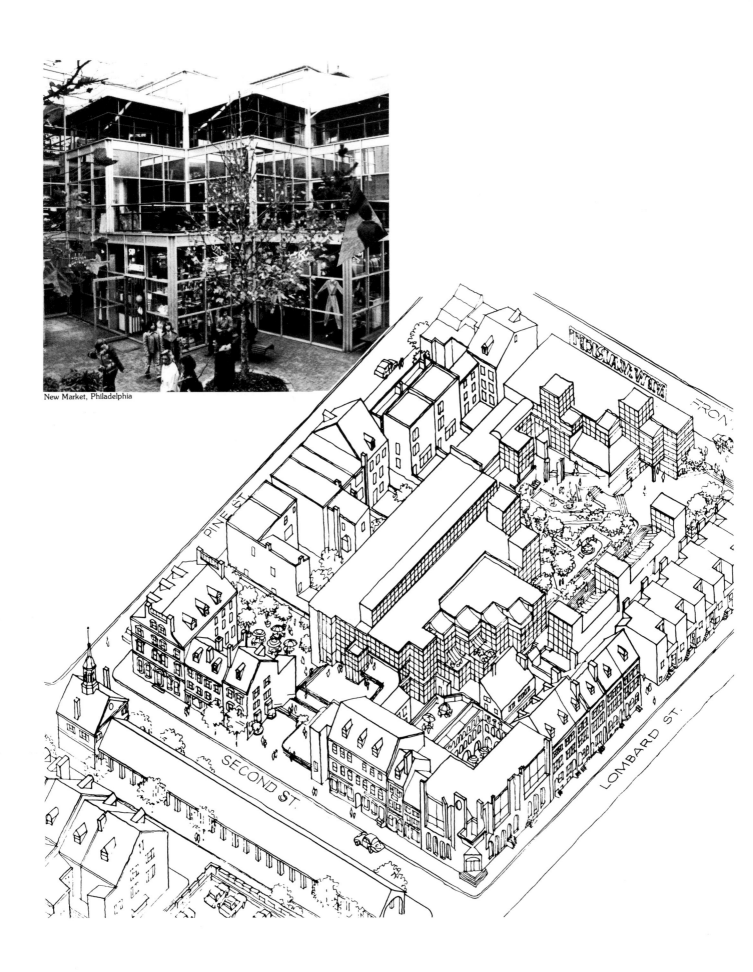

New Market, Philadelphia

THE MARKET

AT CITICORP CENTER

THE SURPRISE OF
SWISS CUISINE
IS ITS VARIETY

THE SURPRISE AT
AUBERGE SUISSE
IS THE VARIATIONS
ON THE VARIETY

AUBERGE SUISSE

Chéz A
Chocolat

HUNGARIA
RESTAURANT

189

St. Peter's Church at Citicorp Center, NYC

190

MAPLE SYRUP

The native Indians of North America knew that spring heralded the sap run of the sugar maple. Legend tells us that a great chief left his tepee as his squaw started to prepare the evening meal, a venison stew. She left it under a broken tree branch, a sugar maple. All day the sap dripped into the pot. When the chief returned, he tasted the stew and named the delicacy "sinzibuckwud", the Algonquin word meaning "drawn from trees".

Some interesting facts about maple syrup - the sugar maple is the state tree of both New York and Vermont. Maple sap contains an average 2-3% sugar. It takes 30-35 gallons of sap to get one gallon of syrup. In the old days, "sugar cabins" were used for boiling down and evaporating the sap. Sometimes the tin evaporators were run continuously for nearly a month.

Cooperation from two Canadian groups has produced some wonderful material for this section. The Indian before the fire and the early Quebec sugarers are from the International Maple Syrup Institute. The drawings of the country scenes are from the Ontario Maple Producers Association.

THE SAP-YOKE.

THE SAP-BUCKETS.

COLLECTING THE SAP.

the Market at Märräkésh

The open air markets of Morocco (souks) have always been colorful affairs — food, clothing, spices, animated discussions in Arabic and Berber dialects.

The architecture is varied and exciting — beautifully carved doors, painted adobe-like buildings, clean white walls broken only by a single window, tents with flags and ribbons sailing out in winds from the Grand Atlas Mountains and exquisite handwork on wooden items and columns.

MATAAM
FEZ

مطعم فاس

Authentic Moroccan Cuisine

Denver, CO

195

G. Clairin

MEXICO

This section is general in nature with most of the art pieces and ideas applicable to all types of promotions, restaurants and decorative treatments.

"Mexican madness" and the timbered ceiling shop interior offer starting points for Mexican arts — a restaurant or gift shop. Sombreros, castanets, bulls heads, hand crafted chairs and brackets are possible advertising and promotional spots.

Estebans

199

© Corporate Image, Ltd. 1978

© CI/aia

Mills, Grains and Bread

Bread, mills and grains are inseparable in graphics arts promotion. The number of new bread and pastry shops sprouting up in major department stores and shopping malls indicates the potential for profit. For example, visit the bread department in New York's Bloomingdale's. You'll see how clean merchandising and visual display can have a real impact on shoppers. Bloomingdale's features bread and biscuits from all over the world — the interwoven decorative wheat breads, Czechoslovakian venoka, Danish cringlers, hot cross buns (which were passed out to journiers in England), French croissants, Arabic pita, panetonne from Italy, hearty rye and glistening pumpernickel from Scandanavia, tiny golden tea rings, apple cakes and marzipan tarts.

Bread can be used in many kinds of retail merchandising: thick rye breads can display slicing knives and silverware; a background panel with two dozen different types of bread attached can merchandise bread boards, butcher blocks and bread slicers; croissants can be placed on beautiful breakfast china for a home furnishing window; and real toast can be used in toasters.

The Bread Bin Shop is natural in look and materials, with plain pine or basswood panels on the wall and plexiglass domes for display. Additional impact can be obtained by painting a stylized loaf of bread on the wall. Shelves can be built into a baker shape that forms a floor stand in a heavy traffic area near the door. The color scheme would range from light beige to golden and deep chocolate browns with jet black for lettering.

The physical form of mills varies with the specific use. Mills were used to grind wheat, saw logs, spin yarn, weave fabric, and even to smelt and forge. Unlike other buildings, mills were usually constructed from within. They often became ungainly-looking affairs, but most were snug, unique and often beautiful.

The English artist James Arnold portrays a postmill. Its body pivots on the center post and when the wind changed, the miller kept the sails into the wind, using the tail poles and secondary wind device. Undershot wheels suited coastal tidemills where water gates trapped the high tide. The undershot and other English mills often worked in the middle of a river where the wheel was pushed in the direction opposite to the water flow.

© Forward Graphics

Mills have a visual richness all their own. Some are clad in wood shingles or boards that "silvered" in the sun . . . others are sturdy structures of native stone and local brick.

A unique dining and shopping specialty center called "The Old Mill" has been launched in Menlo Park, California under the guidance of the L. B. Nelson Corporation of the same city. In the initial conception, the entire facility was built around an old mill in the center of the mall. Its warmth and design influence was extended with the use of some cleverly designed pillar supports and rustic bridges. The mall has as its centerpiece an overshot wheel and a mountain stream flume. The wheel drops the water into the charming stream and the water flows throughout the complex.

The mill theme can also be used effectively in shop displays. Grain measures on counters can add an authentic mill atmosphere and graphic inserts can be designed for inlay areas on the front of counters. Free standing merchandisers can be constructed easily of two standard bases with barrelhead shelves, attached to natural wooden poles and joined at the center. The "miller" sales people can wear French aprons, the burrstone form can be made into a merchandising counter, the wheat sheath form serves as a weathervane, and final decorative touches are a "faked" overshot wheel, hanging sign and sacks of grain leaning against the entrance.

Additional ideas come to mind for graphics and materials for mills. The rich texture of burlap could be used for sign backgrounds, soffit areas and even complete walls. Extra large brass stencils can be attached to the burlap for wall signage or made into a full brass sign and backlit. Stoneware crocks that are so much in vogue today make ideal decor pieces to hold grains and scoops, dried wheat and bearded barley, or flowers.

Wausau Papers

In the full page photograph of wooden display items, the grouping is based on huge wooden spools. Similar to the cable spools seen on power company trucks, they were made expressly for use as furniture.

At the turn of the century, barrel coopers were listed in every city directory, since barrels of all kinds were needed by stores, breweries, mills, and apple growers. Needless to say, the number of cooperage firms in this country today are few and far between. However, there do exist some sources of physical pieces for use in mill promotions. Spaulding and Frost in Freemont, New Hampshire specialize in "coopered" items, including old fashioned lobster and apple barrels, the firkin and sugaring buckets and delightful old-time cheese tubs.

Another excellent source of large barrels and tubs is the firm of Greif Brothers in St. Paul, Minnesota. For additional atmosphere, the photo includes some reproduction milk pails, items from the Jack Daniels reproduction group, a few antiques from the author's collection and penny candy jars that might lend themselves to this type of promotion.

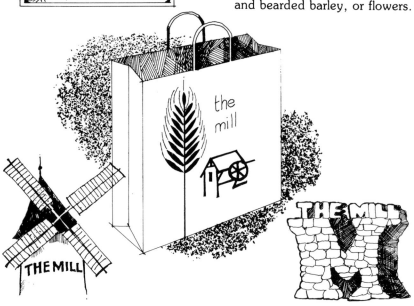

THE SCOOP & BARREL

THE GRAIN BARN

THE Mill

THE Mill

OATS

© Forward Graphics

Saskatchewan
Tourism and
Renewable Resources

204

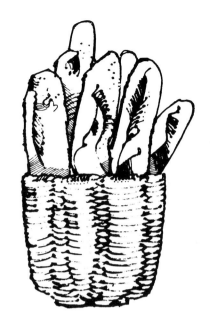

MILL WHEEL

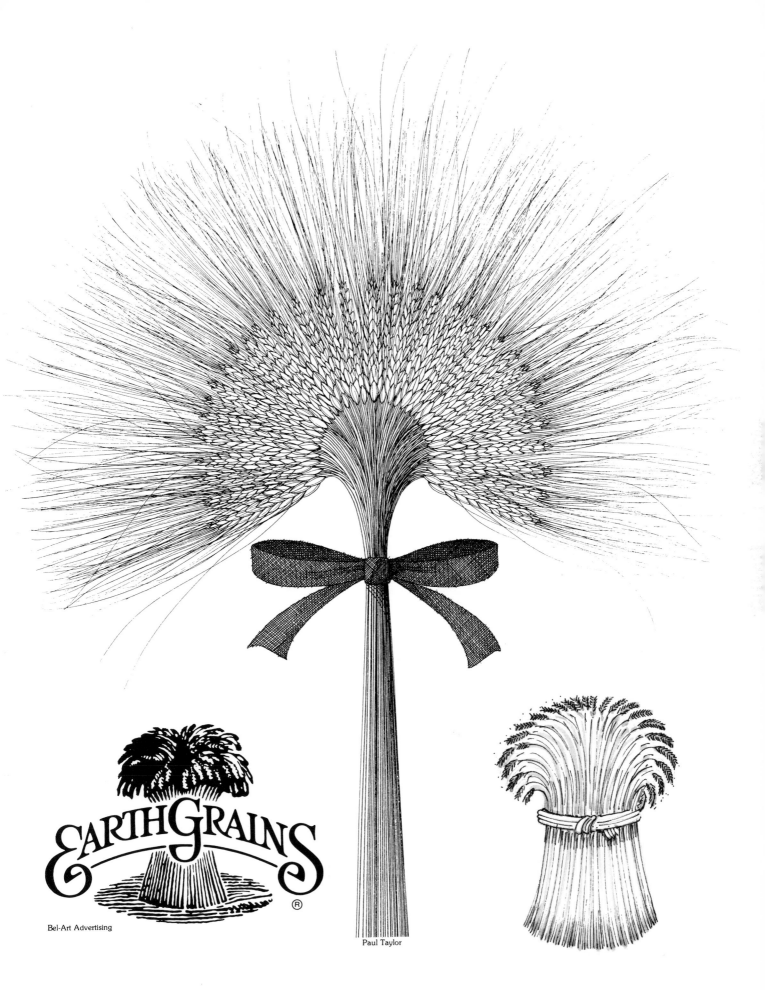

EARTHGRAINS

Bel-Art Advertising

Paul Taylor

Mississippi Steamboats

The Spanish were the earliest explorers, some two hundred years before the French, but the French established colonies at the end of the 17th century. The Louisiana French maintained their dominance in language and continued their easier way of life.

The Southern Louisiana Creole has displayed a remarkable ability to assimilate and "creolize" all newcomers. Originally the term Creole meant any person, regardless of rank or wealth, born in the new world and of pure European heritage. Today, it means an inheritance and a way of life. Cajun, a corruption of "Acadian" was the term applied to their country cousins, "Swamp Billy Creoles", who settled in The Bayous.

Except for New Orleans and a few inland towns, Louisiana was completely rural before 1860. It is from this rural background that we have chosen our theme "The Plantation House" or "The Creole Plantation." The plantation was the focus of all social and economic activities, built both for show and for comfort in the prevailing weather.

The first impression of early Louisiana Creole architecture is not necessarily the accentuated heights of the steeped, hipped roofs. The roof's slopes usually continued without a break to cover the verandas. These galleries extended across the front and often down each side. Early Creole homes, regardless of their pretentions, made use of the available native building material. Practically speaking, there was no building stone in the state. Wood and clay were mixed with spanish moss or deer hair for a "plaster" and near the coast sections, "taddy" plaster was made of ground up shells.

A famous plantation was built in Natchitoches in 1833. It was a magnificent example of the Creole style and on the plantation grounds is the famous "African house". No other similar building exists in the United States. It is a story and a half, brick center building, enveloped and made diminutive, by a huge overhanging roof. The mushroom, beehive appearance strongly suggests homes of some regions of West Africa. Today, it is a museum and its wide eaves no longer provide shelter for wagons or people.

A shop idea incorporates many of the ornate features of the old stern paddlers, including the gingerbread wooden pillars, cotton bales, barrels, boxes, burlap, sawdust, pegged wooden floors. It exudes the general feeling of one of those powerful old boats puffing away up the river. The paddle boats present wonderful opportunities for graphic design, as do the French influenced wrought iron balconies of New Orleans.

The two stunning drawings of steamboats are by Jerry Biederman and were published by the Donald Art Company. The four-stacker side paddler, Francis Skiddy, moved at a terrific rate for that time. The Natchez, with its big boilers, high stacks and extra powerful side paddles, was possibly the best known of the great steamboats.

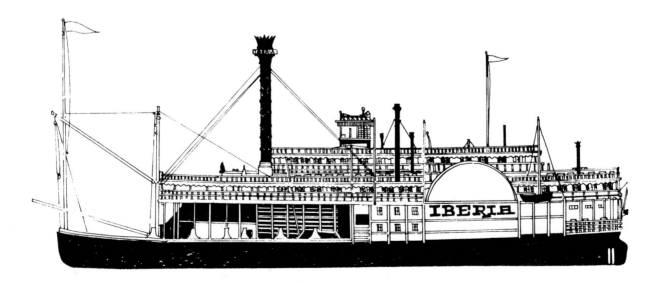

Missouri River Boatman's Shirt

© Folkwear 1978

Schields

HUCK FINN

211

Music

The following pages symbolizing music require absolutely no explanation whatsoever. The area of music and especially the shapes of the instruments and the illustration techniques are countless. The tuba is another magnificent drawing by Paul Taylor and the balance of the pages are devoted to parts and pieces and full shapes of interesting musical instruments.

Exxon Corp. artist John Alcorn

Ludwig van Beethoven.

Johann Sebastian Bach.

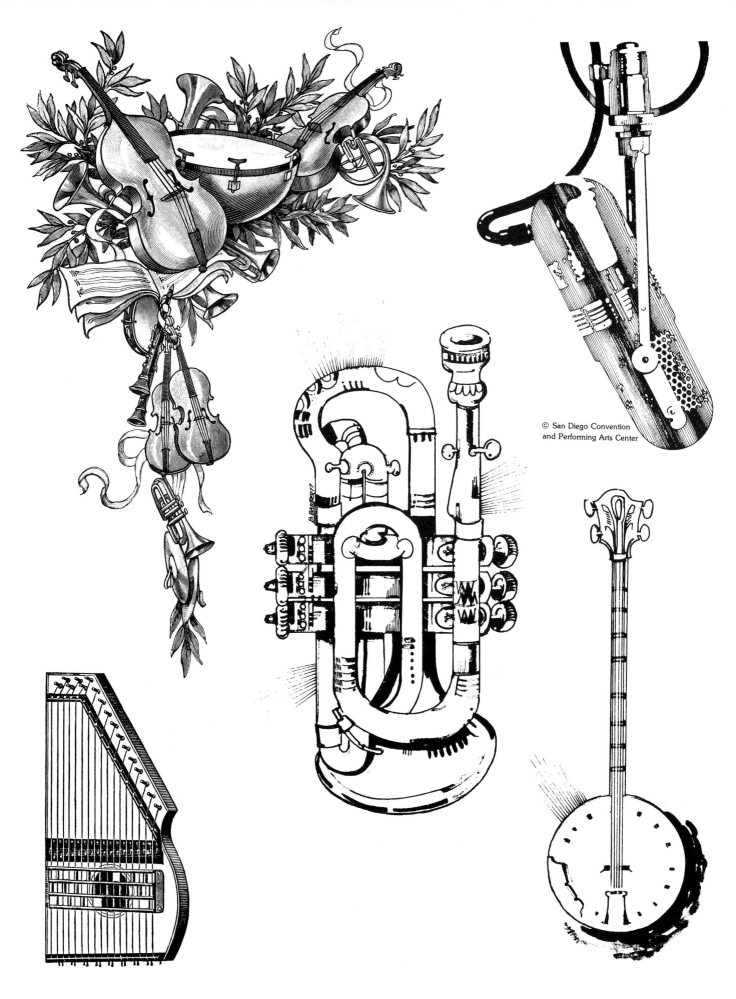

214

Paul Taylor

215

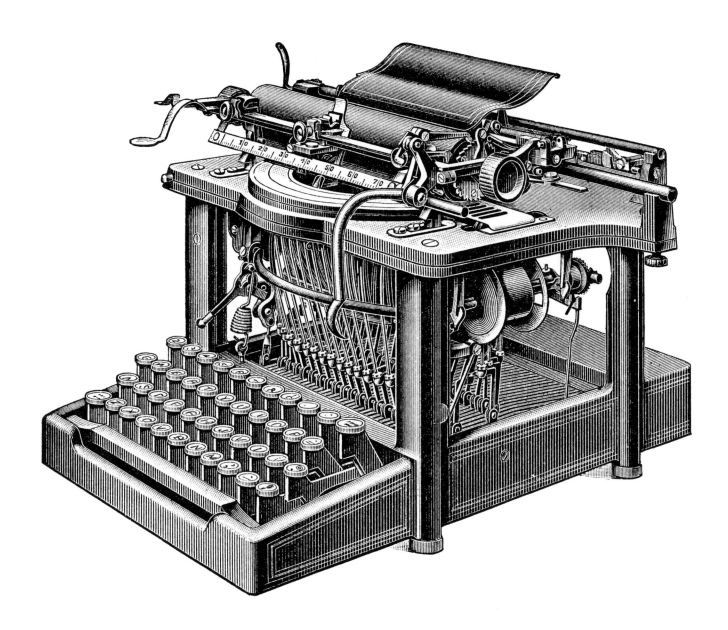

Office Equipment

Typewriters and postal indicia dominate this section with an old-fashioned typewriter as the lead-off symbol. The Pitney-Bowes metered mail indicia has become a generic symbol. It is interesting to see how it has been adapted by designers like Mike Salisbury and Group Four Mail Inc. for their use as letterheads and trademarks.

The section ends with a page of "biggies". These large forms can be real showstoppers as design and display elements in promotion. The key is simple - you merely take a common object and inflate its size. For example, a fiber tube becomes a huge seven foot barrel shaped felt marker.

The approach can vary according to whether the objects are to be constructed in three dimensions or as part of a print campaign. The pencil and marker drawings were used quite effectively by the Rochester, New York paper distributor, Alling and Cory. Claes Oldenburg, the Swedish pop artist, has used this idea to produce outstanding and controversial art pieces, such as his huge lipstick on tank treads at Yale and the baseball bat in Chicago.

The stylized typewriter was a blind embossed piece produced by Beckett paper to publicize one of their paper stocks.

© Pitt Studios

Pitney-Bowes

MIKE SALISBURY
2237
STANLEY HILLS DR.
PHONE
213 656-2248
LOS ANGELES
90046
CALIF.

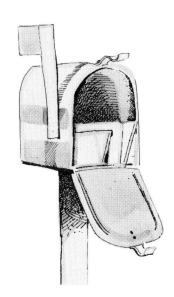

15 EAST BETHPAGE RD.
516/752-7952
PLAINVIEW, N.Y. 11803
G.F.M. 1978

GROUP FOUR
.4
MAIL, INC.

U.S. MAIL
LETTERS

B. BARBER '77

Alling and Cory

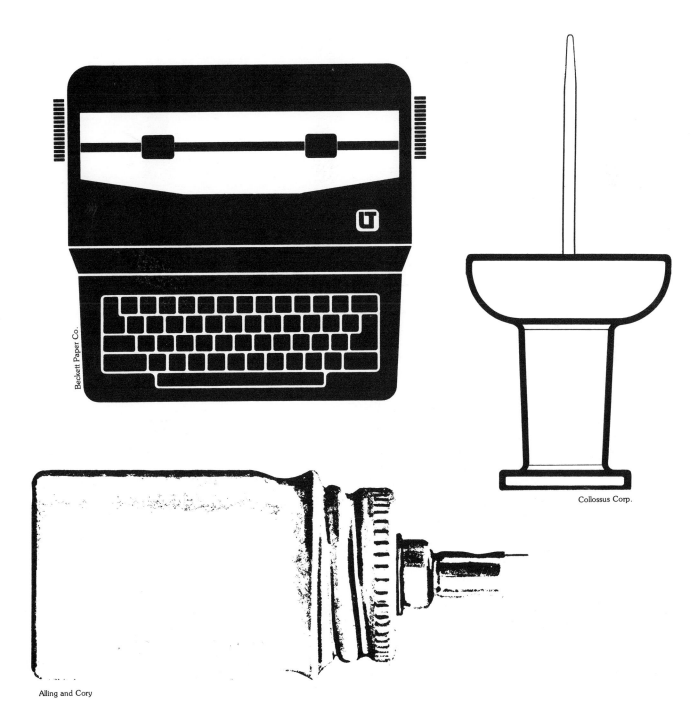

Beckett Paper Co.

Collossus Corp.

Alling and Cory

City Investing Co.

© VOLK

220

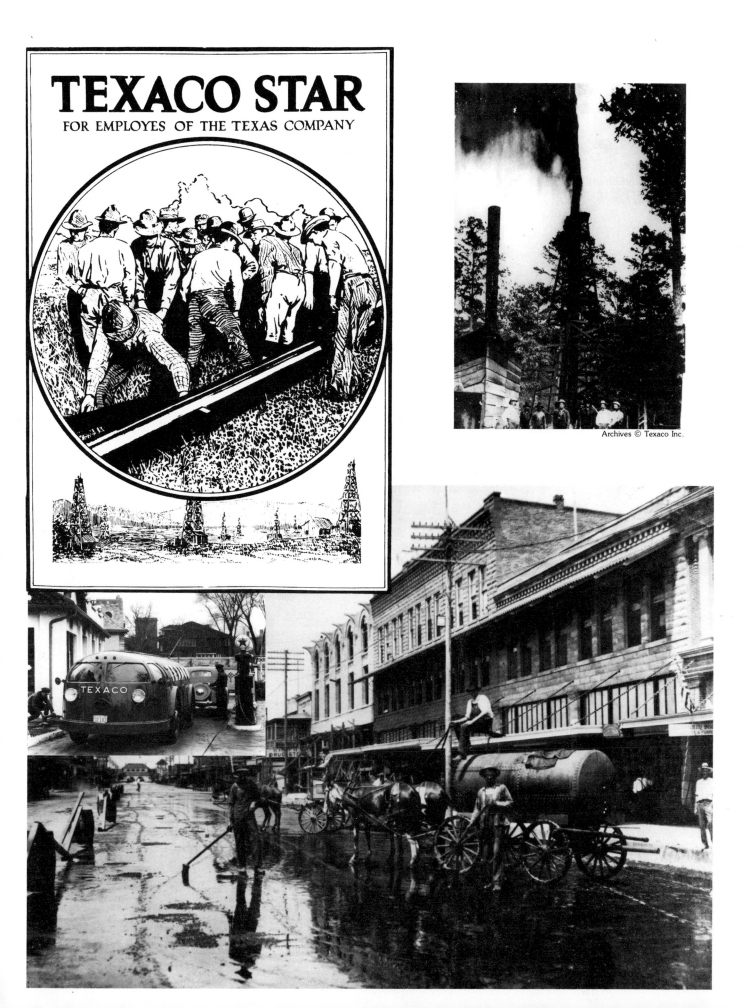

TEXACO STAR

FOR EMPLOYES OF THE TEXAS COMPANY

Archives © Texaco Inc.

1901-1926

With rising prices and shortages, oil has almost become a "dirty word" but it is a necessary evil and is a major subject and symbol in today's advertising and promotion.

The Texaco Star, produced for the employees of the Texas Company, has progressed from an interesting inter-company publication to the slick and interesting public relations production it has become today. The photos are from their archives and are nostalgic and interesting.

1926/1951

1951·1976

Gulf Oil Corp./Pitt Studios

222

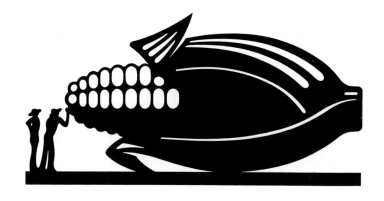

ESMARK

plays cupid in the great American love affair.

ESMARK

expects every gas pump
to earn its keep.

Hardware Age

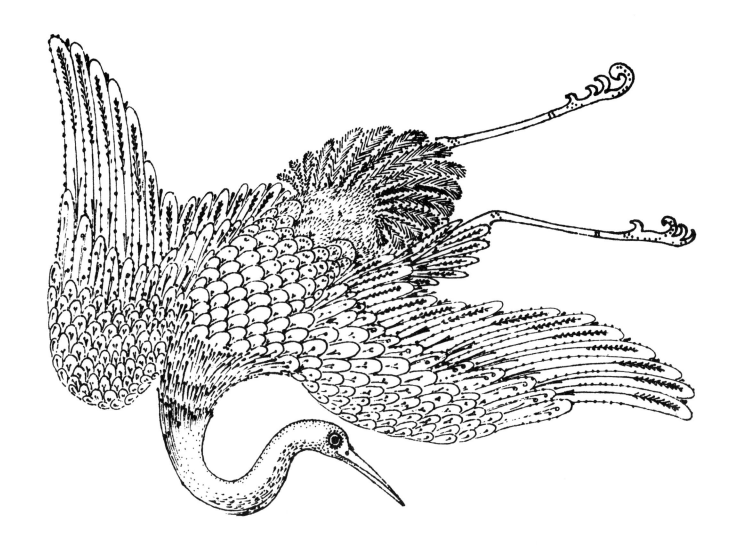

ORIENT
EXPRESS

This section could easily run on for hundreds of pages. These offerings cover just a fraction of possibilities involved in using Oriental influences, motifs and styles in promotion. A soaring bird from Taylor & NG's book on Wokcraft opens this section.

The architecture is varied and interesting. A boutique idea has been styled after a simple ceramic model of a Chinese city square with its tiled roofs and alcoves with banners streaming from long bamboo poles. The Meiji castles of the medieval kings are "stepped" using raw native stones, stucco/plaster like surfaces on the upper elevations and topped with the ever present ceramic tiles. These fortresses were built in this style to discourage assault and often were surrounded with moats and drawbridges.

Japanese shrines with their virile and original style were pure drama. Besides being beautiful, their wide eaves served to protect worshippers from the constant rains. Telegraph size poles of redwood lift the roof high, and local river stones and sand raked in precise patterns contribute to the religious aspects of these structures.

The architectural influences can also be used in restaurant designs and Oriental promotions for retail outlets.

International Paper Company in Portland, Oregon used a new recipe booklet on Mandarin cuisine by Mme. Cecilia Chiang to promote their Long Bell Division kitchen cabinets. Mme. Chiang is an expert in her field as proprietor of the Mandarin Restaurant in Ghirardelli Square in San Francisco.

From the heartland of China, artist James Yeh-Jau Liu has come to the United States to share his style of Chinese brush painting. A graduate of the National Academy of Fine Arts Hangchow China in 1935, today he lives in Tiburon, California.

226

JAPAN

ALFRED PARSONS

Folkwear

JAPANESE KIMONO

JAPANESE FIELD CLOTHING

CHINESE JACKET

CHINESE SKIRT

© Folkwear

© First Colony
Coffee and Tea Co.

Wm. Hengerer Co. artist Pat Banazak

JAPAN TODAY

Tom Kamifuji, Suntory Int'l.

233

© Y. J. Lui

Restaurant Horikawa

Tokyo • Los Angeles • Santa Ana

Tom Kamifuji for Suntory Int'l.

237

CULINARY DISCUSSIONS & ILLUMINATIONS

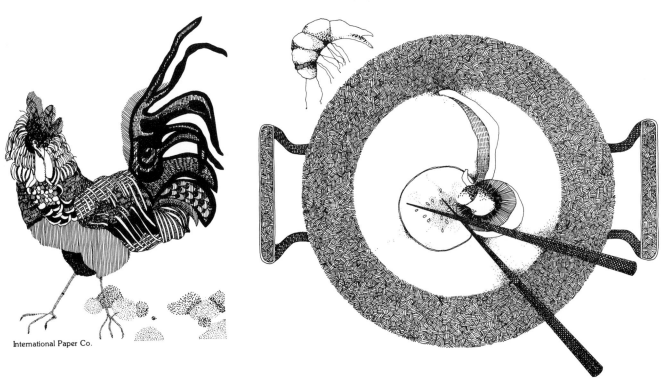

International Paper Co.

239

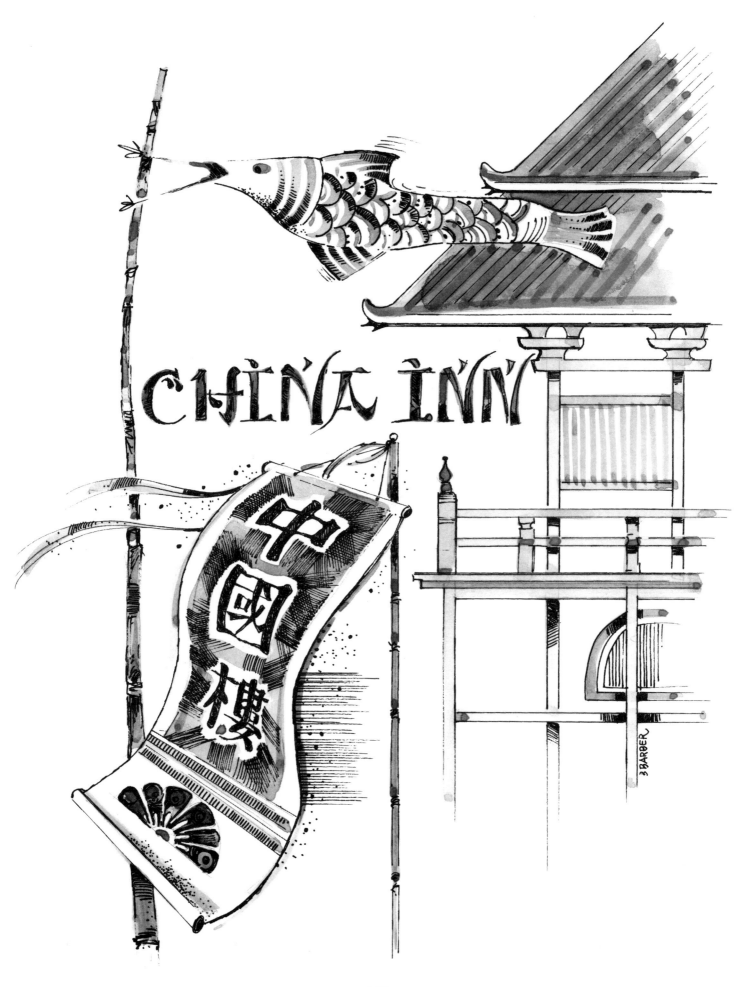

CHINA INN

中國樓

©George Stavrinos

OUTERBANKS

Anything pertaining to an eastern nautical theme can be placed under this category. Off the North Atlantic coast of North America lies a wide continental shelf which extends in some places hundreds of miles from the shore. Large areas form underwater plateaus called "banks." The Grand Banks off New Foundland are part of the system. In New England some areas are termed outerbanks.

Combining the beautiful windblown beaches of the Carolinas and Georgia, the symbols of early fishing and ships gear, and quarterboards, a group of pages are presented using the objects for use in all kinds of promotion and ads.

Christmas in Nantucket utilizes the lighthouse and the art of carving on whales teeth — scrimshaw — has real potential. The term scrimshaw is derived from an old Dutch word — scrimshander — meaning a worthless fellow with too much idle time. It consists of carving and fine line etching on whales tooth, bone or ivory. When completed the design was rubbed with India ink, pitch or lamp black. The scenes often depicted events and dangers, and some pieces are so finely crafted that they are now priced at great worth in whaling museum collections.

Restaurants using the nautical theme abound all over the country, and one of the major suppliers of motif or decor nautical is Kimric Products. A full page of their items is shown for reference.

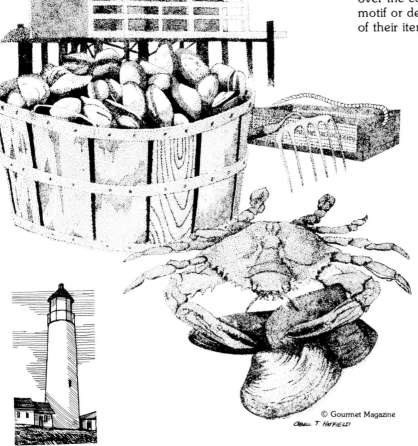

New Brunswick Convention and Visitors Bureau

243

© Cabell Hatfield for Gourmet Magazine

© 1979 VOLK

© 1979 VOLK

CHRISTMAS ON NANTUCKET

TRIMS

GIFTS

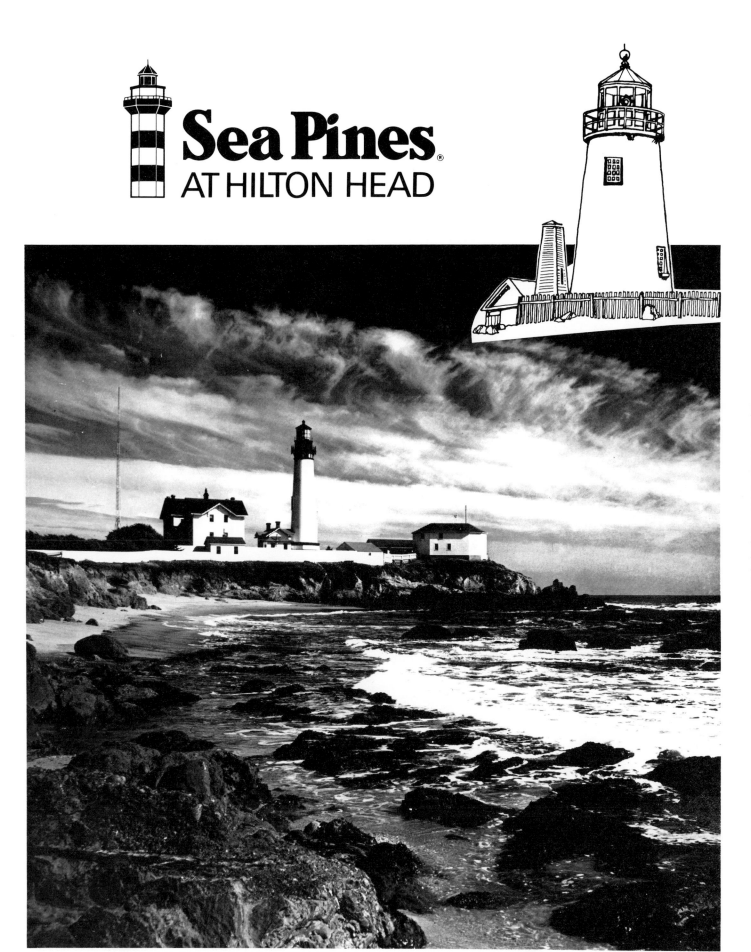

Sea Pines.
AT HILTON HEAD

Freelance Photographers Guild

1OR1535

The Marlinspike Sailor
© Hervey Garrett Smith
John de Graff Inc.

© S.T. Preston & Sons artist Carolyn Blish

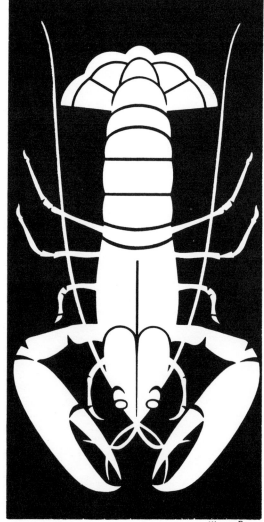

THE SCRIMSHANDER

by William Gilkerson

The Nautical Ivory Worker and
His Art of Scrimshaw, Historical and Contemporary

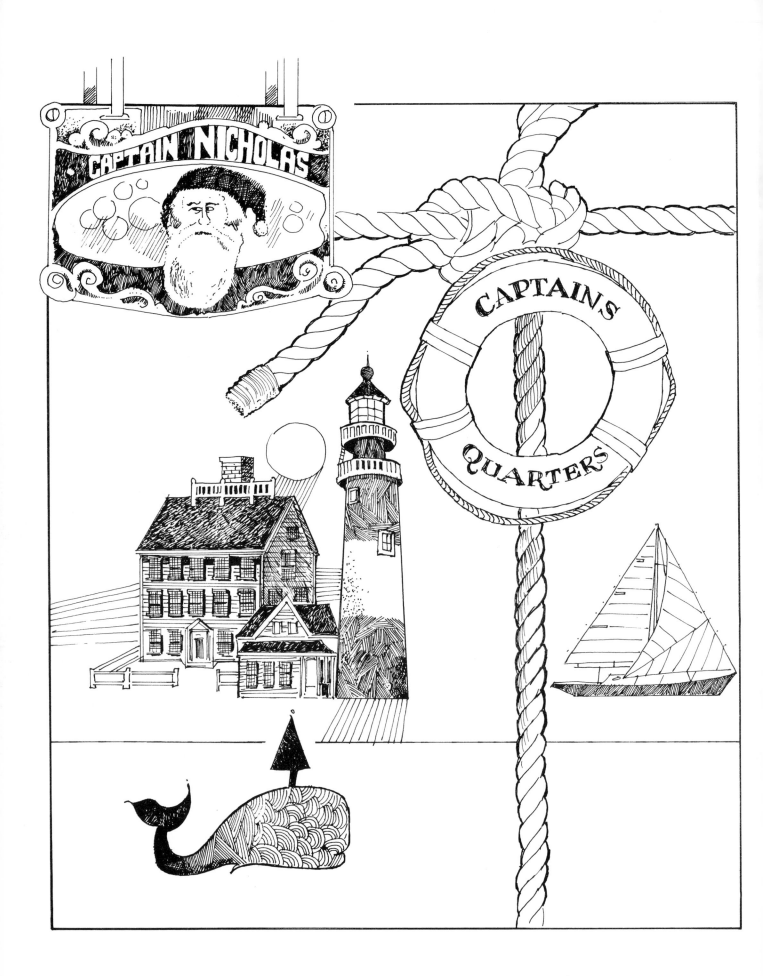

249

Pennsylvania Dutch

The definition of "peasant" as indicated in dictionaries, is a "class of person, chiefly European, who tilled the soil as small landowners or as laborers." Of the many influences on the American retail scene, certainly "peasantries" has to be counted as one of the most significant. Witness the couture designers fascination with these styles. The anthropologic interest in it and the impact of the television series, "Roots," all combine to re-establish our basic wishes to remember our origins and to continue the folk ways of the past.

Collecting folk art, lessons in craft skills and the resurgence of international institutes in major cities underline the movement. Beautiful original designs can be found in a variety of objects. Wonderfully detailed washboards and household implements handcarved from Hungary and the Balkans, bobbin lace from

Holland, wooden birds from Portugal, paper mache from Mexico, Amish scratch design eggs from Pennsylvania and the wonderful art of Pysanky, hand decorated eggs from the Ukraine. All contribute as a wonderful source of inspiration for designers.

Researching early Czechoslavakian costumes, we were pleased to find the wonderful Batik like fabrics made by 19th century peasants.

It was found that the technique had been handed down for generations, originating in the unusual dying methods used by tribes in Nigeria. Specific areas of the cloth were painted with a "resist" material in folk art shapes, including hearts and rams, flowers and countless other simple, beautiful forms.

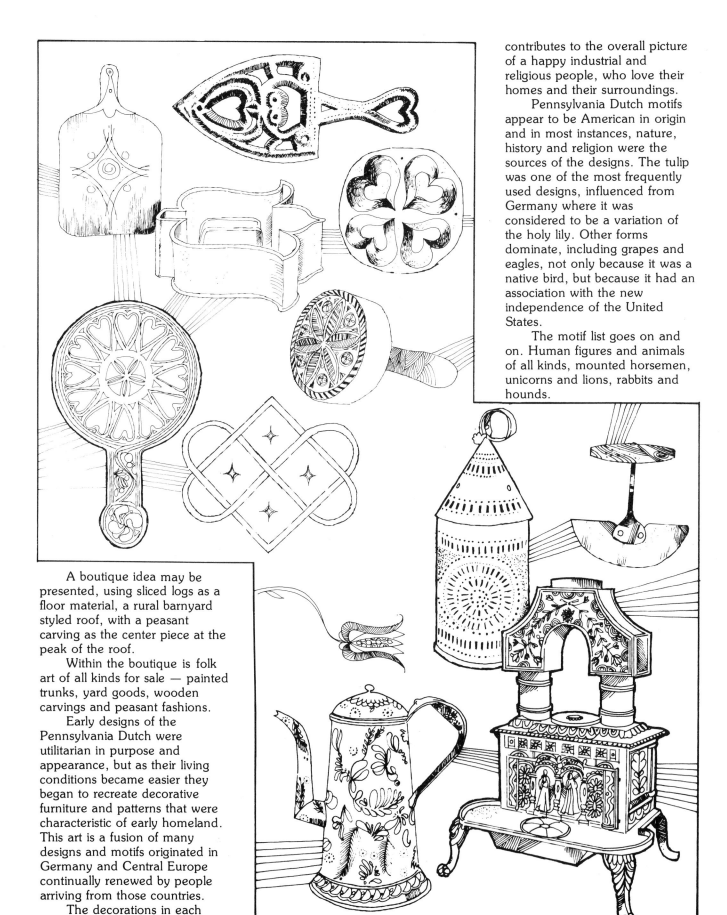

contributes to the overall picture of a happy industrial and religious people, who love their homes and their surroundings.

Pennsylvania Dutch motifs appear to be American in origin and in most instances, nature, history and religion were the sources of the designs. The tulip was one of the most frequently used designs, influenced from Germany where it was considered to be a variation of the holy lily. Other forms dominate, including grapes and eagles, not only because it was a native bird, but because it had an association with the new independence of the United States.

The motif list goes on and on. Human figures and animals of all kinds, mounted horsemen, unicorns and lions, rabbits and hounds.

A boutique idea may be presented, using sliced logs as a floor material, a rural barnyard styled roof, with a peasant carving as the center piece at the peak of the roof.

Within the boutique is folk art of all kinds for sale — painted trunks, yard goods, wooden carvings and peasant fashions.

Early designs of the Pennsylvania Dutch were utilitarian in purpose and appearance, but as their living conditions became easier they began to recreate decorative furniture and patterns that were characteristic of early homeland. This art is a fusion of many designs and motifs originated in Germany and Central Europe continually renewed by people arriving from those countries.

The decorations in each house on chests, toys and chairs

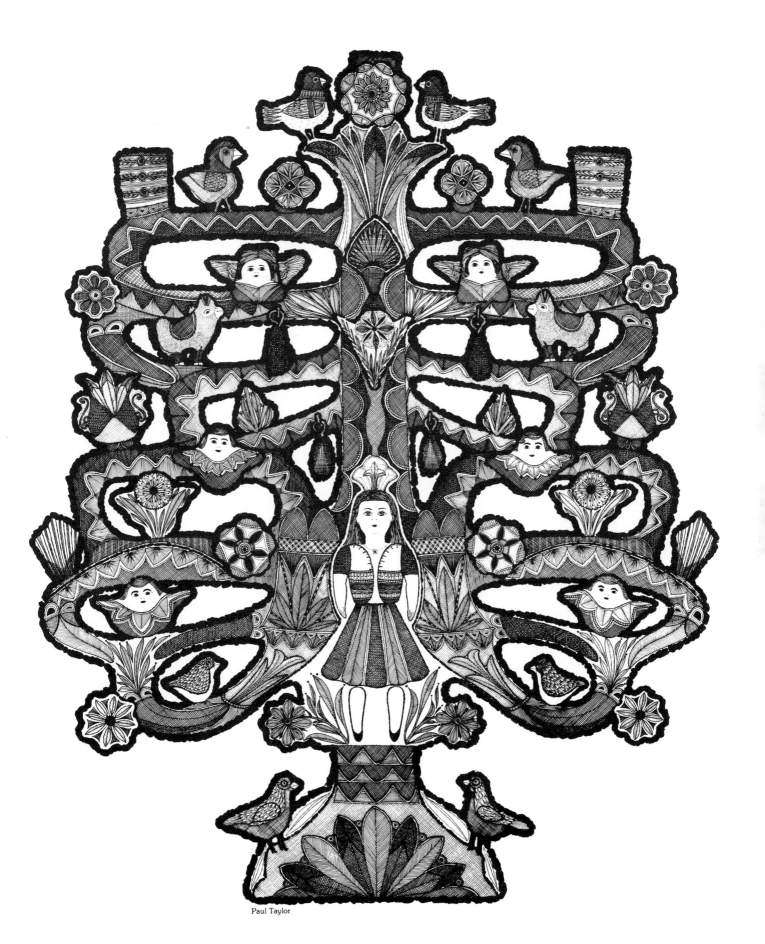

Paul Taylor

PRINTING

In his book, "Connections," James Burke lists the invention of moveable type as one of the most significant in our civilization. It took the production of books and manuscripts from the laborious, handwritten stage to mass production of printed matter.

With Gutenberg and his colleagues, we have the "beginning communication" followed with the inventions of the wireless radio and television.

The early presses were similar to those used by Ben Franklin, with which he produced his early "Poor Richard's Almanac" and printing has progressed through the centuries from wood cuts and steel engravings to lithography.

The days of handset type are sadly coming to a close with the advent of the new photographic lettering machines, but from the standpoint of richness, look and pure simplicity, nothing can match the beautiful wooden type that was "standard" at the turn of the century. Combining this beautiful old type with the multi-compartmentalized drawers called, "California type cases," one finds beautiful inspiration for display and photographic backgrounds.

They have great potential for the craft industry and most specifically for the collector of miniatures, as they make ideal wall hangings to carry the small and detailed miniatures that are so much in vogue today.

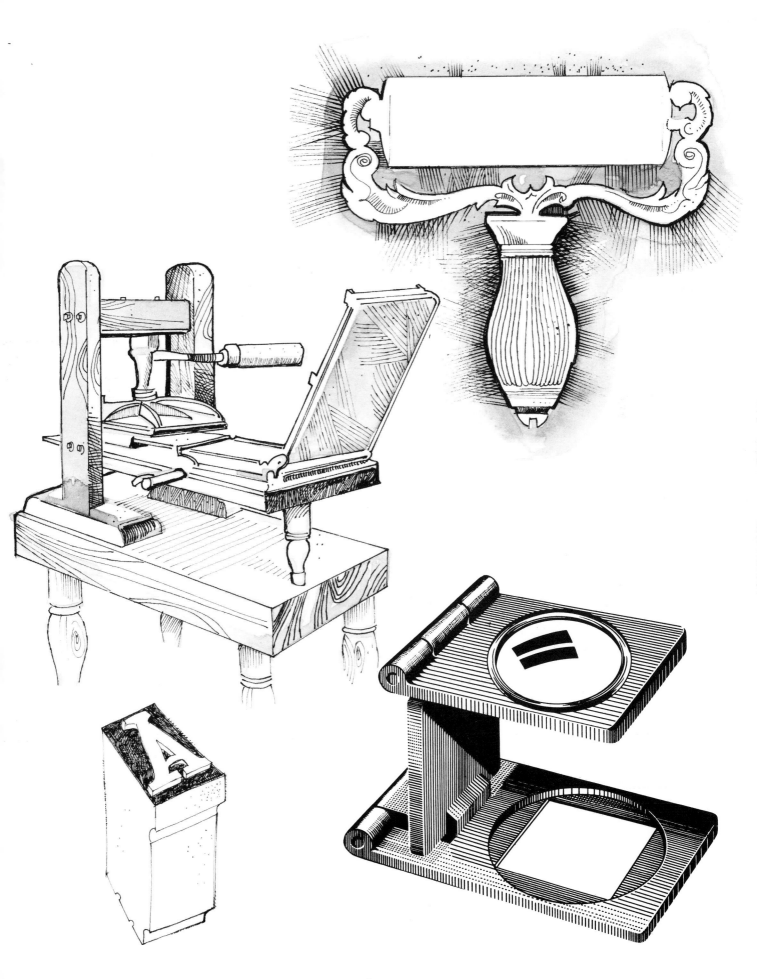

Recycled Buildings

A valuable movement came from that unforgettable national celebration, the 1976 Bicentennial. In their effort to contribute something of value to this anniversary, hundreds of cities, towns and states, thousands of private citizens and business enterprises set about cleaning and restoring old houses and buildings. Many structures achieved local, regional, and national status as "preservation quality" and today the National Trust for Historic Preservation in Washington serves as the headquarters for all of the local boards.

In their efforts to restore these pieces of valuable property, many people have sought sources of authentic materials with which to bring these structures back to their original status. Firms specializing in reproducing these materials have flourished. One of the major firms producing urethane reproductions of decorative materials is Focal Point in Georgia. Others, like San Francisco Victoriana and Cumberland Woodcraft, produce actual wooden items for interior and exterior restoration. Welsbach Lighting has always supplied authentic lamps and now is experiencing a resurgence of interest in these oldies.

John P. Wilson has held his famous Architectural Antique Auctions for 10 years each June in Los Angeles. He has been editorialized in Fortune magazine, Time and The Wall Street Journal as an amazing entrepreneur in the unusual field of architectural antique sales. The 10th Annual Auction brochure (the catalog is $25) lists $10,000,000 worth of antiques in dozens of categories. Several listings are as follows — Tiffany glass windows, a Burton ales pub from England, the Newport, Kentucky drugstore, and a complete greenhouse.

The Olentangy Management Company of Columbus has become involved in a unique residential restoration development project to restore over 200 homes in Dayton, Ohio. Mary Rae and Associates offered a set of prints depicting unique homes in Denver that was used as a promotional program. An illustration of their own building has been used to great advertising advantage by Finch, Pruyn and Company. This section ends with a Bruce Buttes drawing of the famous Belli Building in San Francisco.

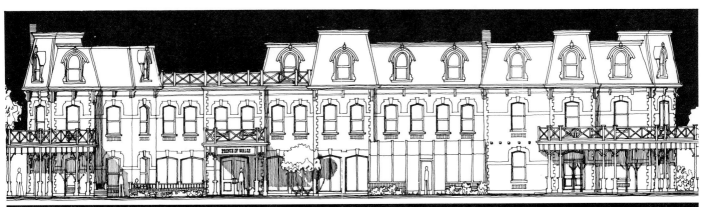

Prince of Wales Hotel
Old Fort Niagara, Ontario

257

© Trolley Square, Salt Lake City

258

GAZEBOS

WELSBACH

Since 1877

260

San Francisco Victoriana

"The Finest in 19th Century Architectural Products"

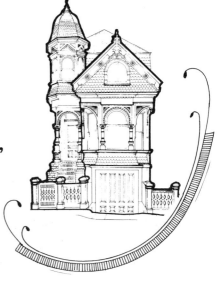

Brass and Bronze
Hardware

Anaglypta
Wallcovering

14 Patterns

Antique Embossed Wallpaper Borders

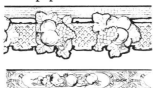

Original 1890's Stock

Plaster Ceiling Centerpieces

47 Designs

Fireplace Mantels

Plain and Fancy Designs

Wooden Staircases

Rails, Balusters, Posts and Caps

Plaster Ceiling Cornices

Plain and Fancy Designs

Wainscot and Trim

Complete Assemblies

Plaster Wall Brackets

20 Designs

Fancy Fret Work

Authentic Designs In Solid Oak

Reproduction Lighting Fixtures

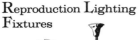

31 Designs

Cast Iron Spiral Staircase

4 ft. and 6 ft. Diameter Modular Units

Fancy Cedar Shingles

6 Patterns

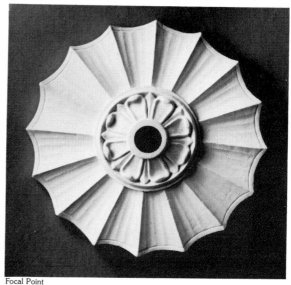

Focal Point

GINGERBREAD

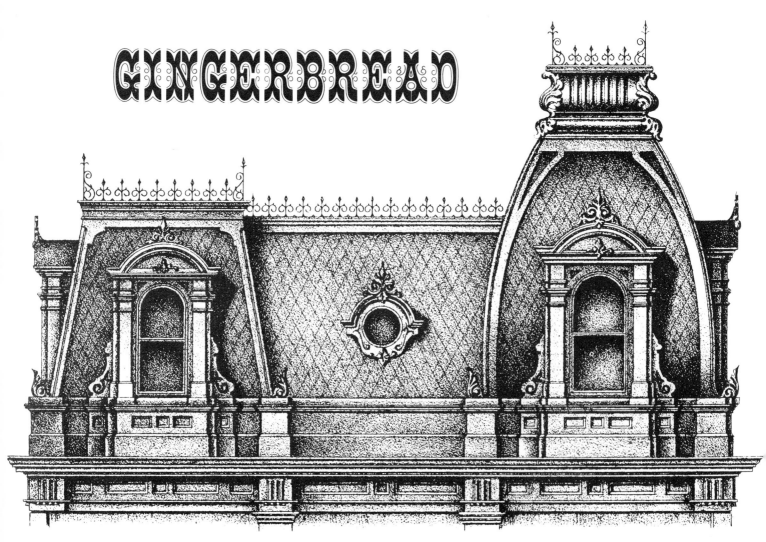

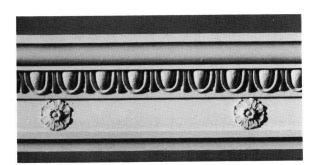

Focal Point

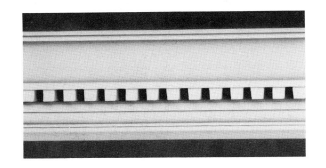

© Trolley Square, Salt Lake City

263

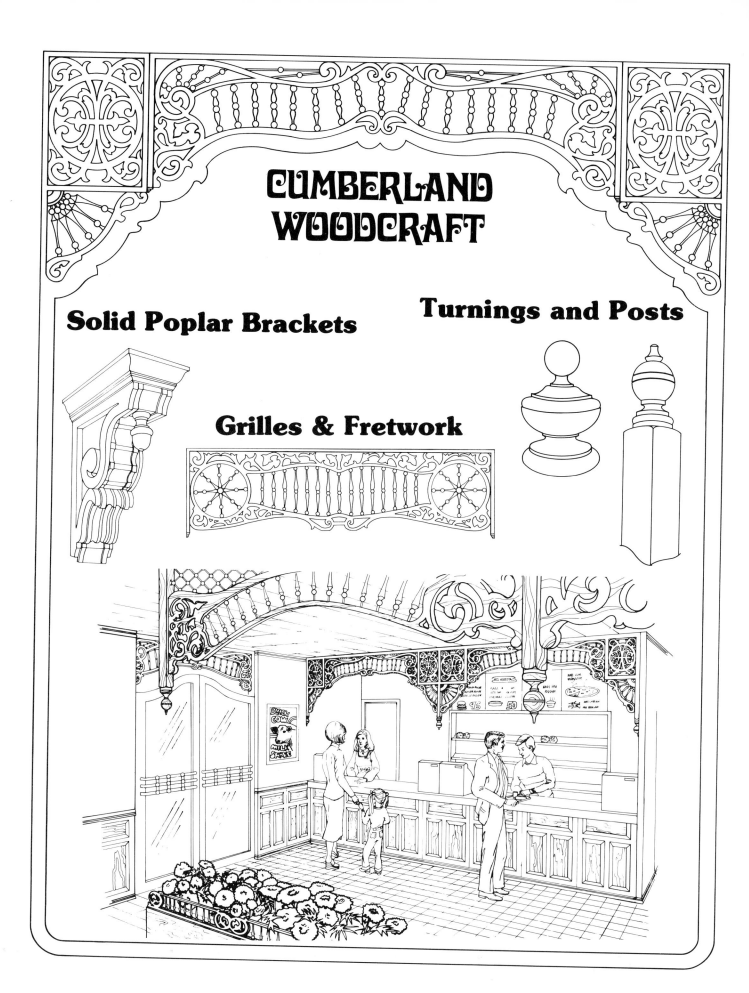

CUMBERLAND WOODCRAFT

Solid Poplar Brackets

Turnings and Posts

Grilles & Fretwork

Exterior Spandrel and Brackets

Decorative Grille and Fret Partitions

Fret Brackets

Medallions

Spandrel Line

Cumberland Woodcraft

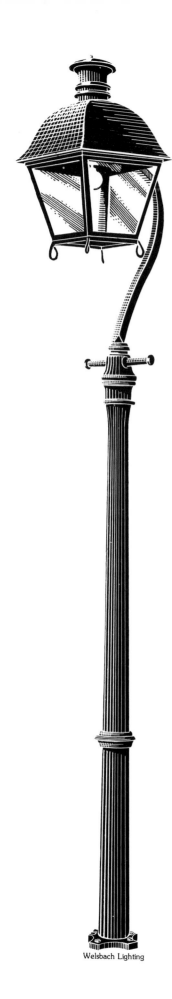

Welsbach Lighting

Finch, Pruyn & Co.

266

ARCHITECTURAL ANTIQUE AUCTION

10TH

Freelance Photographers Guild

268

HESDORFER/78
Copyright 1978 Mary Rae & Associates, Ltd.

Copyright 1978 Mary Rae & Associates, Ltd. HESDORFER/77

269

HERITAGE PLACE
·A SAN FRANCISCO ANTIQUE HERITAGE·

Renaissance

Renaissance

Olentangy Management Co.

271

RESTAURANTS

A potpourri of restaurant trademarks is presented in this section. It starts with two New York City landmarks — the classic Luchows, followed by the famous Windows on the World.

Putsch's in Kansas City adorns its menu with line drawings of the beautiful fountains on the Plaza. Dick Sommers illustrates for Signature magazine's restaurant reviews. A variety of material is included in the remaining pages.

Lüchow's

© Inhilco Inc.

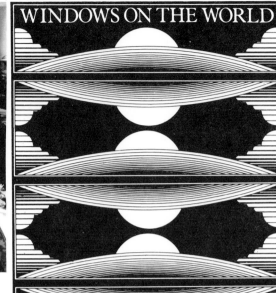

WINDOWS ON THE WORLD

The Hors d'Oeuvrerie

Ernie's, San Francisco

Putsch's, Kansas City

healthworks!

THE SALAD COMPANY

Pittsburgh

Healthworks

W.D. Crowley's, Atlanta

© 1977 Downside Risk

280

Lee and Mary Sievers

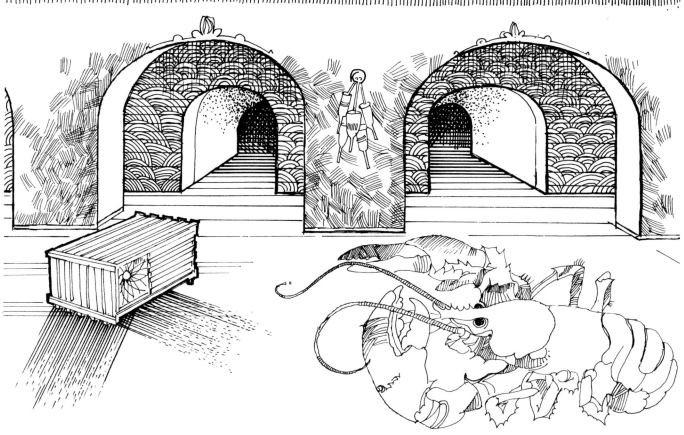

Kelly's

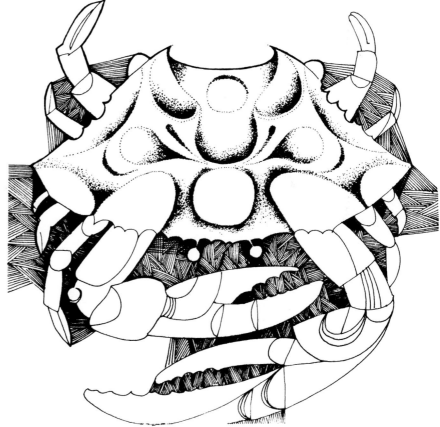

SHUCKERS

Signature Magazine artist Dick Sommers

La Ronde

RESTAURANT

Cincinnati

Airport Marina Hotel artist Jack Unruh

CHARCUTERIE EXTRAORDINAIRE · PATISSERIE · BOULANGERIE

PIRET'S

Ⓣ

Ciao

© Spectrum Foods Inc., San Francisco

Hilton, Atlanta

Chicago

Las Palmas Inn

Orlando

THE BOOJUM TREE

At the Doubletree Inn • Southcenter

Seattle

Whales Tale Restaurant

666 FRONT STREET
LAHAINA, MAUI, HAWAII 96761

TUTTLE'S

Coral Gables

HARRY'S BAR
and American Grill

© Spectrum Foods Inc.

Junior's
Levison and Sacks Advertising Inc.

Begue's
RESTAURANT AND PATIO

WHEN IS IT BEST TO BEGUE?

Sunday Buffet Brunch celebrates unusual foods and elegant potables with a guitar for dessert.

Creole Tuesday Buffet Luncheon is a feast of jambalaya, gumbo, red beans, dirty rice and other New Orleans' specialties.

Friday's Catch is a lavish seafood luncheon buffet, so fresh you can almost smell the salt air.

Begue's Dinner is an experience in French cuisine and Old World service unmatched anyplace except the Old World.

Lunch at Begue's is an everyday love affair with the French Quarter, from giant 3½ oz. martinis to celestial omelets & splendid salads.

Reservations 586-0300

ROYAL SONESTA HOTEL

The 510, Minneapolis

© Forward Graphics

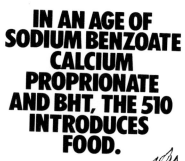

Boca Raton

The 510, Minneapolis

Clethro's

Chianti
© Spectrum Foods Inc., San Francisco

MacArthur Park

RESTAURANT SYMBOLISM

B BARBER.

CRACKERS

John Q's
Public Bar & Grille

Signature Magazine artist Dick Sommers

Sup, sip, sample, discern, nosh, nibble, munch, crunch, imbibe, indulge, share, splurge, gorge, gormandize tonight.

Cheese Cellar®
Restaurant & Bar
125 E. 54 · 758-6565

Cheese Cellar®
Restaurant
125 E. 54th St.
758-6565

© Wyse Advertising

290

RETAIL

Serendipity

Serendipity is "the faculty of happening upon fortunate discoveries when not in search of them."

This grouping covers trademarks, building and retail illustrations, unusual interior treatments, space ads and canvas totes — all retail related and all interesting.

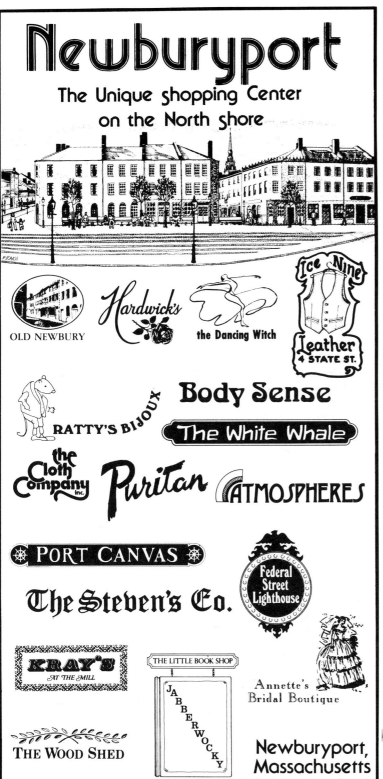

Newburyport
The Unique shopping Center
on the North shore

FRAKE

OLD NEWBURY

Hardwick's

the Dancing Witch

Ice Nine
Leather
4 STATE ST.

RATTY'S BIJOUX

Body Sense

The White Whale

the Cloth Company inc.

Puritan

ATMOSPHERES

⚓ PORT CANVAS ⚓

The Steven's Co.

Federal Street Lighthouse

KRAY'S
AT THE MILL

THE LITTLE BOOK SHOP

JABBERWOCKY

Annette's Bridal Boutique

THE WOOD SHED

Newburyport, Massachusetts

Produced by the Newburyport Chamber of Commerce with cooperation of Essex County Tourist Council of Massachusetts, Inc.

People at NorthPark like to watch people at NorthPark.

BLT

DANSK
INTERNATIONAL DESIGNS

BAZAAR DEL MUNDO

San Diego

irma's bag

Photos courtesy Greetings Magazine

Toni Totes

293

© Bergdorf Goodman

294

Barrett Hill Inc.

rooftops

This may prove that a different view or perspective on any subject is an interesting way to set up a promotion or ad.

The mini-section opens with an aerial view of one of the roofs of Curacao in the Netherlands Antilles. It could be the start of an island promotion, "the Willemstad shop" or "the Dutch Attic."

Huge rooftop vents and fans could be used as mannequin props for retail windows and of course those famous ceramic pipe stacks in Paris could make an excellent photography background — "The Rooftop Studio."

297

RUSSIA

This is a slice of early Russia — a Russia starting in the 13th century when the Mongols appointed Prince Yuri of Moscow as the Russian Grand Prince. In 1613 Michael Romanov became Czar, starting the Romanov line that would rule until 1917.

The symbols of sovereignity were jeweled caps with gold and sable. Bright gleaming samovars, crystal vodka glasss, royal Easter eggs, hand-painted children's toys, onion domes on wooden churches and troika bells ringing clearly in the midnight air as a sled cut briskly across a frozen lake.

The Pullman firm at 200 South Michigan in Chicago produced a fine series of black and white institutional advertisements in association with the U.S.S.R. business firms they were cooperating with in a joint venture. Their artwork opens this section.

ТЯОІКА

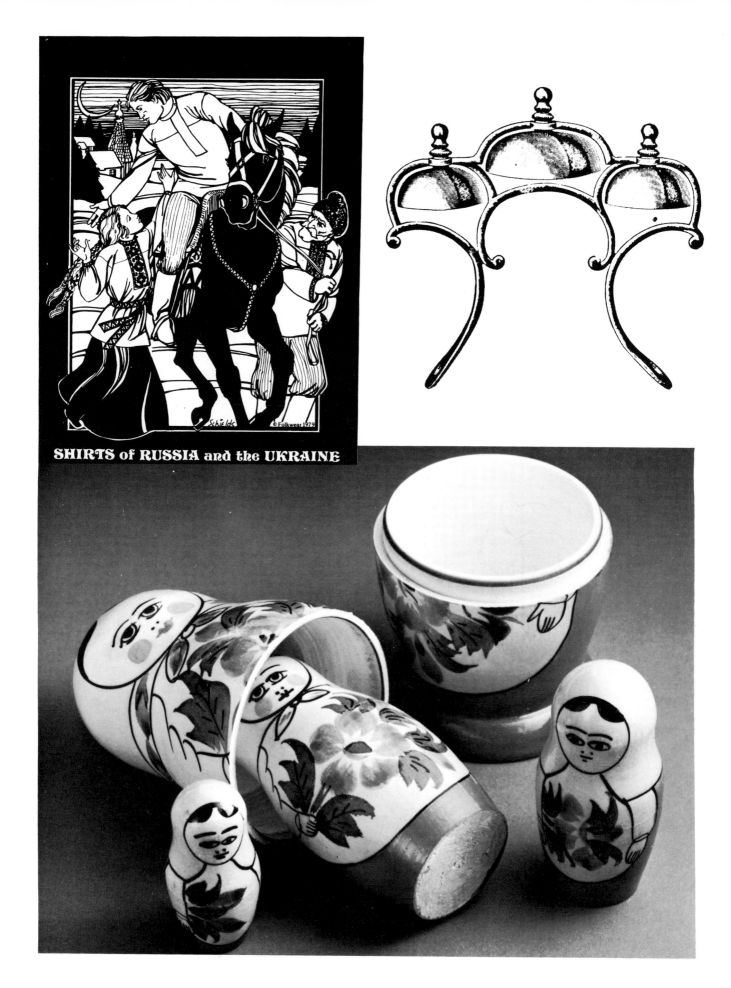

SHIRTS of RUSSIA and the UKRAINE

RAMBERT

SEASONS

JANUARY					
FEBRUARY					
MARCH					
APRIL					
MAY					
JUNE					

The most obvious holidays are the big ones — New Years, then Lincoln and Washington's birthdays, Valentines Day, Easter, Mother's Day, Father's Day, Fourth of July, Labor Day, Halloween, Thanksgiving and Christmas. But what about those minor days that would make great promotions — like the first night that baseball was played under lights at Ft. Wayne, Indiana (June 2, 1883)? And a real "biggie," the day the first adhesive postage stamps in the United States were introduced by a private mail service in New York (February 15, 1842). The list goes on and on. Local promotions can be centered around a symphony or zoological garden drive, the birthday of a local dignitary, plus any number of local ethnic holidays and special occasions.

This section starts with an interesting chart of seasonal artwork from one of the Clip Services. Harry Volk used different art techniques to symbolize the months of the year.

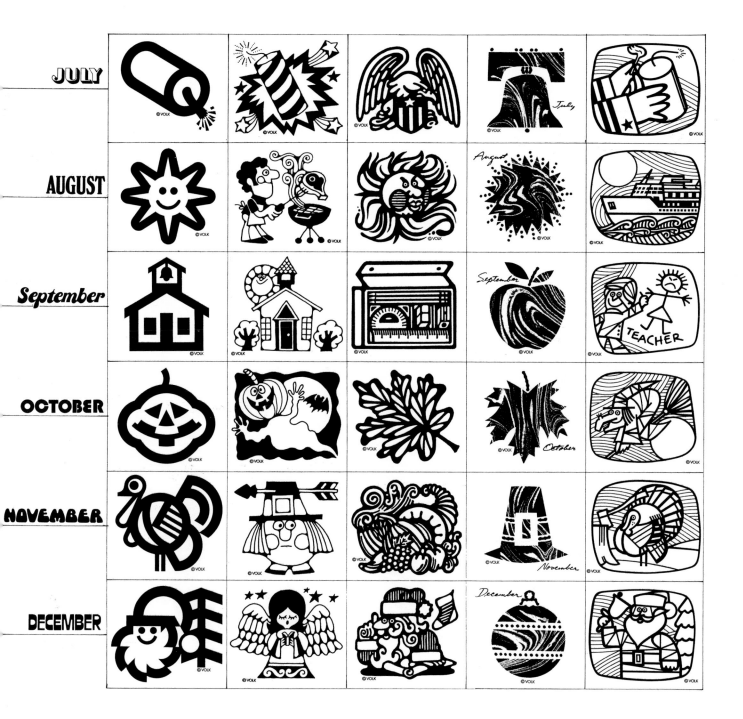

©VOLK

308

© Williams-Sanoma

bruce barber

© Ontario Ministry of Industry and Tourism

Shops and Signs

This section needs little explanation. It includes some shop exteriors which can also be erected inside retail stores as walls in two dimensions. Paul Taylor is represented with his excellent tavern sign and page of symbols. The balance of the work is free of text — the ideas stand on their own.

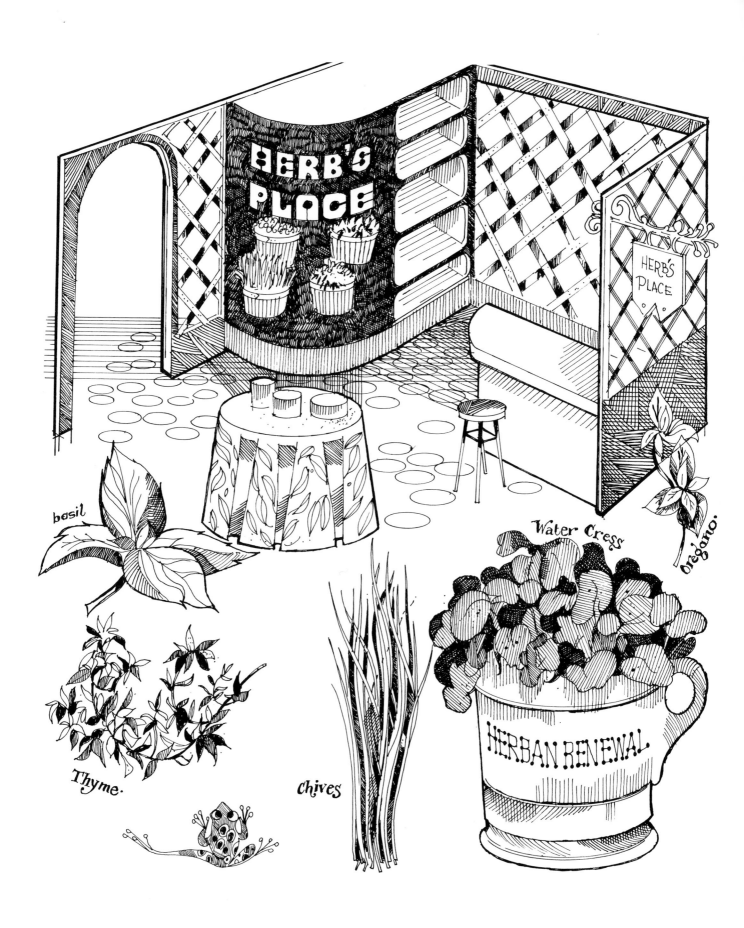

HERB'S PLACE

HERB'S PLACE

basil

Thyme.

chives

Water Cress

oregano.

HERBAN RENEWAL

blueberry patch

flutterbye

bee keeper

grass roots

B·BARBER·

313

court terrarium

NORSK

Wild Mushrooms

TURTLE BAY

CAT TAILS

radish red

Franco American Confetti

le creperie

HUB BUB

Christmas Mouse

little orphan jeans

the neon chicken

niftie

fertile delta

the glass apple

Summer

315

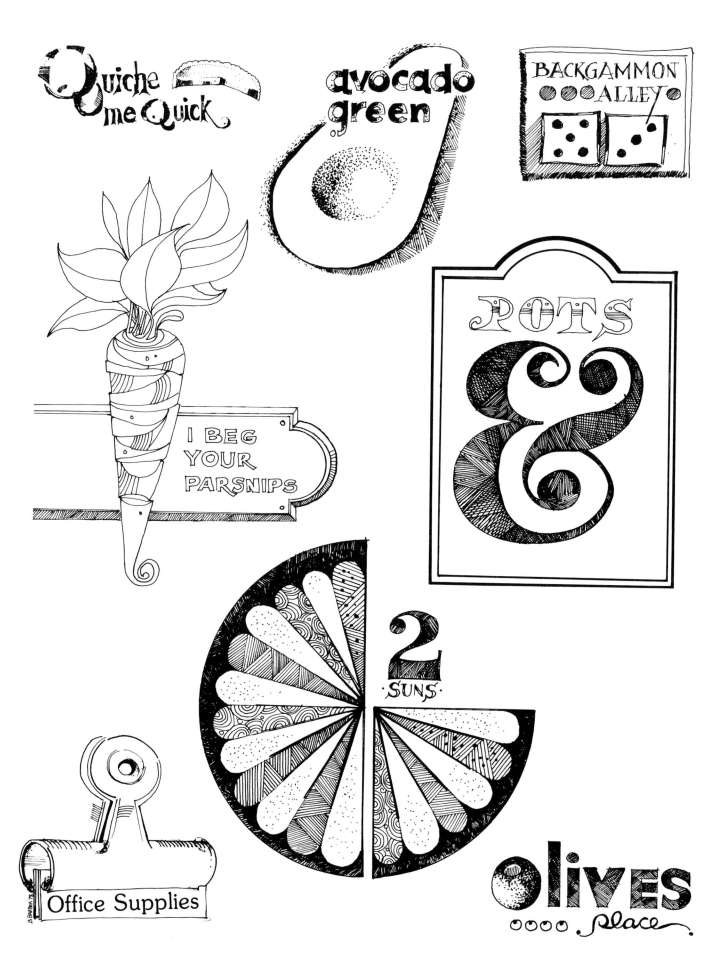

Quiche me Quick

avocado green

BACKGAMMON ALLEY

I BEG YOUR PARSNIPS

POTS &

2 SUNS

Office Supplies

olives place

316

CLOTHES FOR **TADPOLES**

Kid Stuff

if you need me...just whistle!!!

LYONS

THE RED CRAYON

SILVER SKATE KEY

ACORN

GRAB BAG

SNUG AS A BUG...

Easy as...

the pickle and the mustard seed

The Golden Lemon

THE Hobby HORSE

Father's Day

two markets

French MARKET

Pierre's

FISH

eels

CRABS

Via Veronica

320

THE LOFT

CASEY JONES

bills
bagel
bakery

the Peak

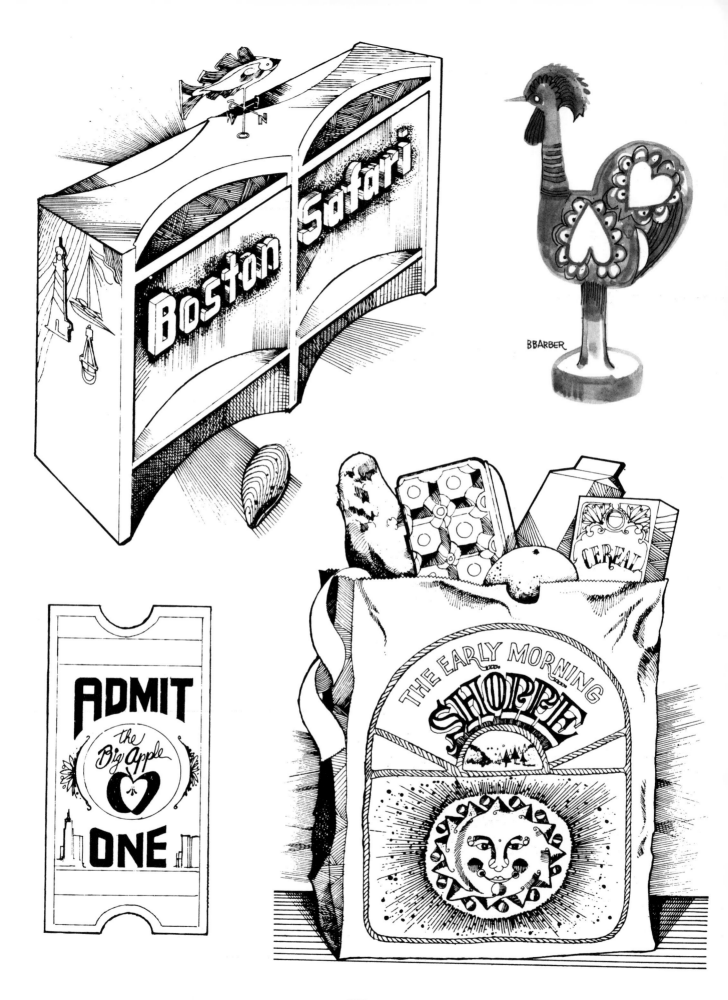

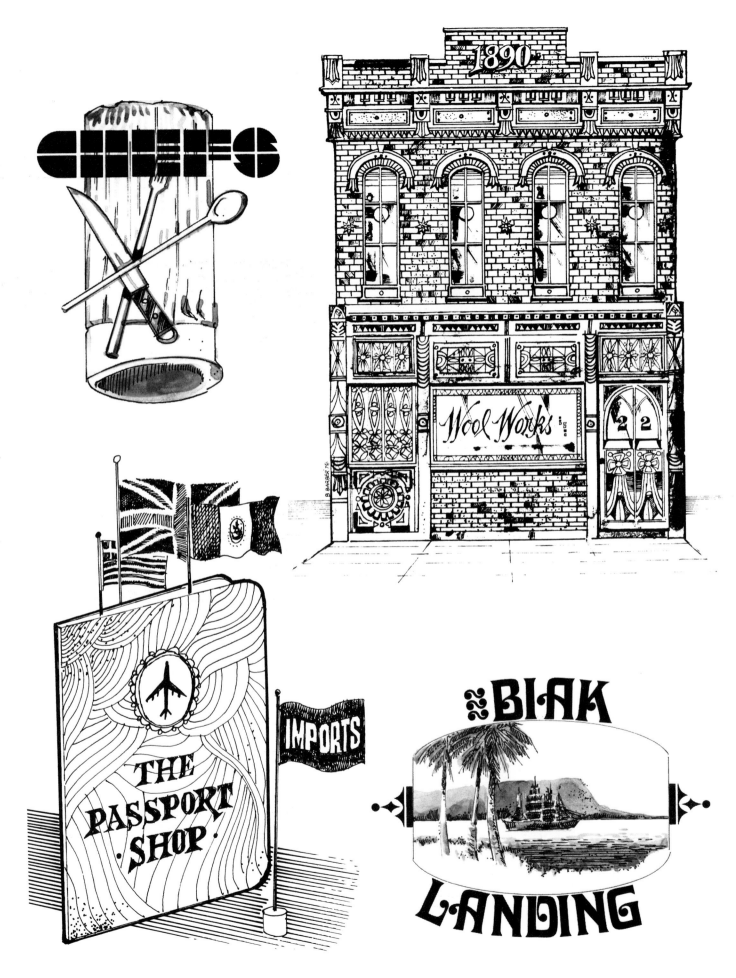

CHEFS

1890

Wool Works

2 2

B. BARBER 76

THE PASSPORT SHOP

IMPORTS

BIAK LANDING

Show Biz

FLICKS

TICKET
2
★★★

STAR

TAKE
STUDIO
1
3

324

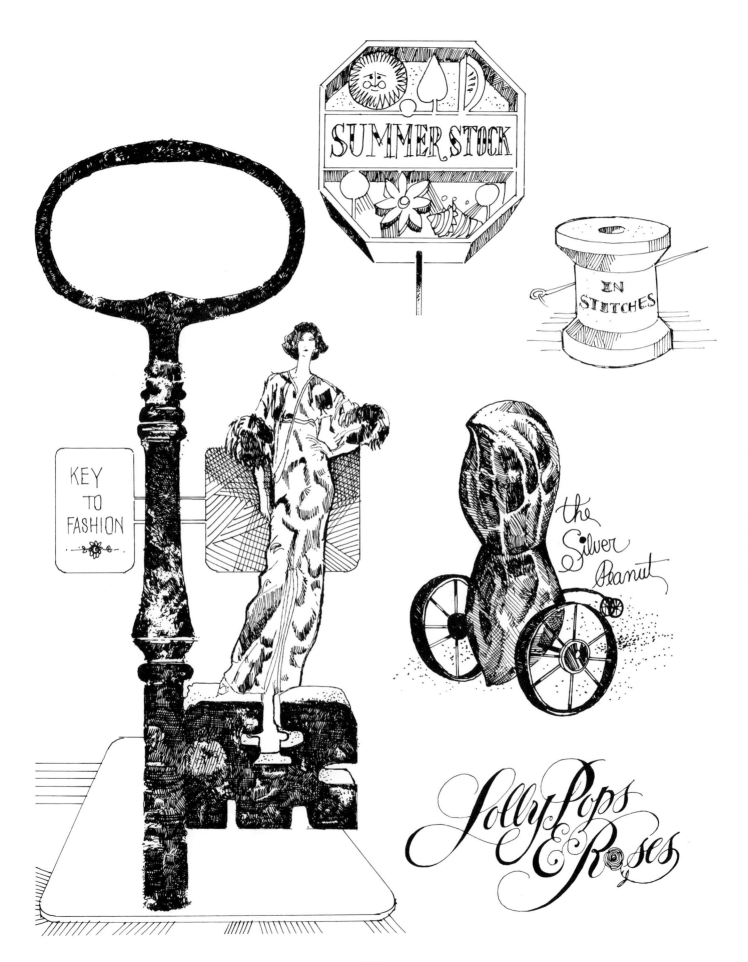

SUMMER STOCK

IN STITCHES

KEY TO FASHION

the Silver Peanut

Lolly Pops & Roses

Paul Taylor

1776

TAVERN

Paul Taylor

Silhouette

Marvin Simmons

SIL OO ET - an outline drawing filled in to resemble a shadow. A person seated between a lighted candle and a piece of paper on the wall — this simple method of illustration is always powerful. Everything is reduced to the simplest of forms and the technique has wonderful decorative possibilities. Etienne de Silhouette, a Frenchman, was responsible for creating this form of portraiture.

Marvin Simmons of the Lehigh University Art Staff has used silhouettes in his work to publicize different events. The Esmark series uses the technique in the truest sense — making sure the edges are sharp and the highlights and detail drawn (or were they cut?) accurately.

Pacific Coast Builders Conference

© Live Steam, Cadillac MI

OUTDOOR
TRADERS
INCORPORATED

HABERSHAM PLANTATION

Taccoa, GA

The Second Annual Lehigh Green Grass Folk Festival, sponsored by the Lehigh Student Activities Committee and Sing Out Magazine. Featuring Rosalie Sorrels; the Bottle Hill Boys; Paul Geremia; Martin, Bogen, and Armstrong; Grant Rogers; Alice Gerrard; Honey Boy Edwards. Grace Hall, Lehigh University, Friday and Saturday, April 13 and 14, at 8 p.m. Tickets, $2.50 for each performance, or $4.00 for both, available in Bethlehem at Lehigh Student Activities Desk, Lehigh University Bookstore, and the Renaissance; in Allentown at Upper Story and Music Scene; in Easton at Not Just Another Pretty Face. Free workshops Saturday morning and afternoon in front of the University Center.

Marvin Simmons

Alaska
(ANC) just 6 hours

Calgary
(YYC)
just 4¾ hours

Las Vegas
(LAS)
50 minutes nonstop

Reno
(RNO) 1¼ hours nonstop

(YVR)
2½ hours nonstop
Vancouver

Acapulco
(ACA) 3½ hours nonstop

San Francisco
(SFO) 1 hour nonstop

Mexico City
(MEX) 3¼ hours nonstop

Hawaii
(HNL) 5½ hours nonstop

Salt Lake City
(SLC)
1½ hours
nonstop

Guadalajara
(GDL) 2¾ hours nonstop

Phoenix
(PHX) 1 hour nonstop

Don Weller for Western Airlines

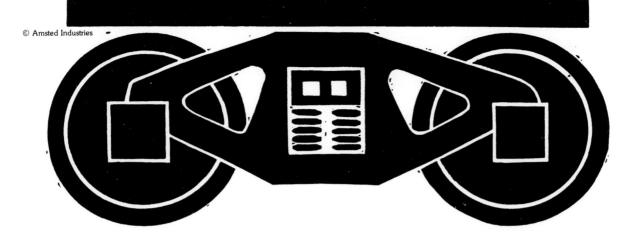

Marvin Simmons

SAINT NICOLAS

Hear a cantata by Benjamin Britten celebrating the hero-saint at 3 P.M. Sunday, April 20, in Packer Memorial Church at Lehigh University. Performers will include the Lehigh University Glee Club and Chamber Singers, Chatham College Choir and the Orchestra of the Mostovoy Soloists. John Aler will be tenor soloist with Robert Cutler conducting. Shorter works by Holst will be performed. Sponsor is the A. N. Cleaver Memorial Fund. Admission is free.

ESMARK

views sandwich-making as a noble art.

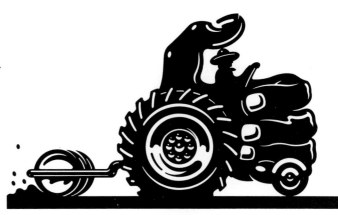

Not the prosaic slice of something between two slabs of bread, but an imaginative arrangement of Deli treats from Esmark's food company, Swift. Cheeses, sausages, loaves, roasts, hams, specialty meats, poultry, prepared foods. With Deli desserts to follow. Deli—one of the fastest-growing branches of the food business. Growth is what Esmark is all about. In food, fuel, fertilizers, financial services, family products. Write for information. Department CFR, Esmark, Inc., 55 East Monroe Street, Chicago, Illinois 60603.

ESMARK

has a vested interest in the American cheeseburger.

Sources

The Chicago Creative Directory is a comprehensive listing of over 3000 companies involved with communications in the Chicago area and ten surrounding states. It is a desktop reference - 8½ x 5½ hardcover with lay-flat spiral binding. The major categories are Photography, Illustration, Color Separation, Audio Visual, Production, Sound and Music Studios, Post Production Labs, Equipment, Talent and Advertising, Marketing and Public Relations Services.

Inquiries should be addressed to The Chicago Creative Directory, 333 N. Michigan Ave. Chicago, IL 60601. (312) 236-7337.

Creative Source 1981/82 is a luxurious hardbook reference totaling 352 pages. The table of contents lists "The Best of Canada" in Photography, Stock Photography, Photo Labs, Illustration, Graphic Design, Graphic Services, Film, Audio Visual, Exhibit & Display, Screen Printing, Printing, Color Separation, Typography and Special Services.

The source book contains 1018 color and 385 black and white photographs and illustrations. If you appreciate creative excellence and nice juicy references, you'll enjoy this one. It is a gallery of visual beauty from cover to cover.

Creative Source is published annually by Peter Cordy. Write to Wilcord Publications Limited, 501 Eglinton Avenue East, Suite 203, Toronto, Ontario, Canada M4P IN4. (416) 487-4762/63.

The 1981 Creative Black Book is the eleventh edition of the world's leading directory of commercial talent and suppliers. The new edition is in two volumes and packaged in a sleek, sturdy, black slipcase, making it easier than ever to find the best and brightest in international talent.

There are ten sections of the book consisting of over 300 beautiful 4-color ad pages and 21,000 free and accurate listings from both the United States and Europe. One of these sections lists and showcases the work of illustrators, graphic designers and others specializing in creative services.

A tightly controlled free distribution has put the 1981 Creative Black Book in the hands of 20,000 creative people in every major ad agency in Western Europe and North America. Another 19,000 copies have been bought worldwide.

In order to be listed in The Black Book, a request must be submitted on letterhead before June 15th, specifying in which section the listing should appear. The 1981 edition may be purchased by sending a check or money order for $40.00 (includes shipping and handling). Friendly Publications, Inc., 401 Park Ave. South, New York, NY 10016.

The Graphic Artists Guild in New York City produces a directory of illustrators and designers, which they claim to be the largest single reference book in the country. The directory presents its members' work, including that of Robert Rodrigues, Milton Glaser, Bart Forbes, Doug Taylor and many others. Over half the pages are in full color. There are 20 color spreads and 200 advertising pages. The black and white pages are equally impressive with the fine work done by well known book, newspaper and editorial illustrators, hand letters, etc.

The sections are as follows: Illustrations - 150 pp., Graphic Design and Lettering - 48 pgs., Textile Design - 37 pp., Artists' Representatives - 16 pp., Photography, Retouching and Production - 12 pp. Also, twelve pages are devoted to the activities and functions of the Guild. The directory is produced approximately every other year and is distributed free to a limited number of qualified art buyers.

The circulation is 5,000 directories with a small number sold to members and non-members (1981 price $25.00 to members -$35.00 to non-members). The directory is a non-profit, cooperative venture - produced at cost and paid by the advertising members in the book. Direct inquiries to D. K. Holland, Graphic Artists Guild Directory, 30 E. 20th Street, New York, NY 10003.

RSVP is an illustrated directory of freelance illustrators, designers and photographers.

Richard Lebenson and Kathleen Creighton, co-publishers of RSVP, announced recently that their new edition (RSVP) has undergone a name change. Formerly The Directory of Freelance Talent, RSVP 6 has broadened its horizons to encompass all areas of creative resources. RSVP is now available to art buyers and the general public nationwide. Copies may be purchased at most art supply stores or by contacting: RSVP, P.O. Box 314, Brooklyn, NY 11205. The price is $12.95/copy.

The 1981 RSVP puts art directors in touch with illustrators and photographers, production studios and graphic designers. It showcases the latest work of some of the nations best-known talents and introduces many of the most creative newcomers in the field. RSVP has 209 fully illustrated pages, over 235 individual full-color reproductions and a unique 24 hour answering service that puts art buyers in touch with many of the hand-picked, carefully screened artists featured in the book.

sports

Powder Mountain — a hypothetical ski resort begins the sports group — followed by a few logo and sign treatments. Then some real life resorts with big recognizable names — Snowmass and Aspen.

The balance of the work shows how versatile styles can be — from the illustrations for a sports equipment ad to crisp line engravings for First Day Olympic Mail.

snowmass

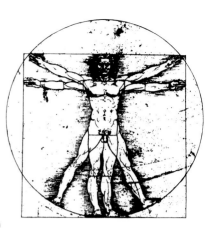

Aspen

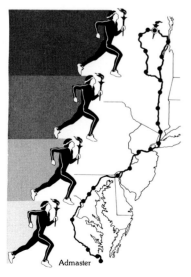

Admaster

THE
OPENING
CEREMONIES
FOR THE
1980
WINTER
OLYMPIC
GAMES
FEBRUARY 13, 1980

RON MACKENZIE

San Francisco

Eddie Bauer ®

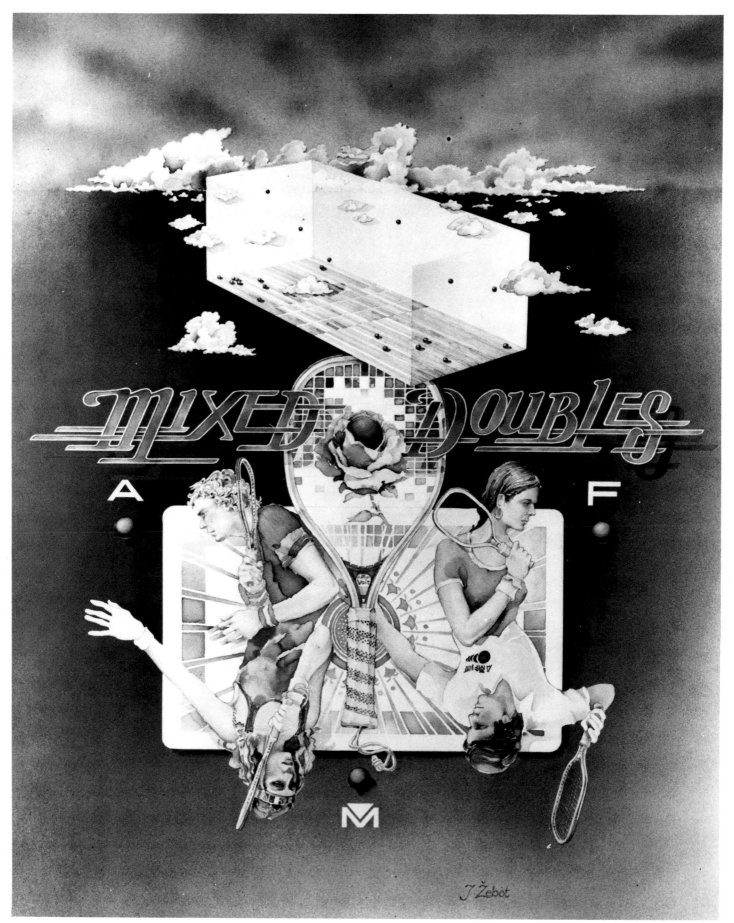

J. Žebot

Airport Marina Hotel artist Jack Unruh

© United Airlines

© San Diego Convention
and Performing Arts Center

340

Atlanta

THE MEADOWLANDS
HILTON
Meadowland Parkway
off Route 3

Dick Sakahara

THE ACTION MAN SLACKS ☐ THE ACTION MAN SLACKS ☐ THE ACTION MAN SLACKS ☐ THE ACTION MAN SLACKS

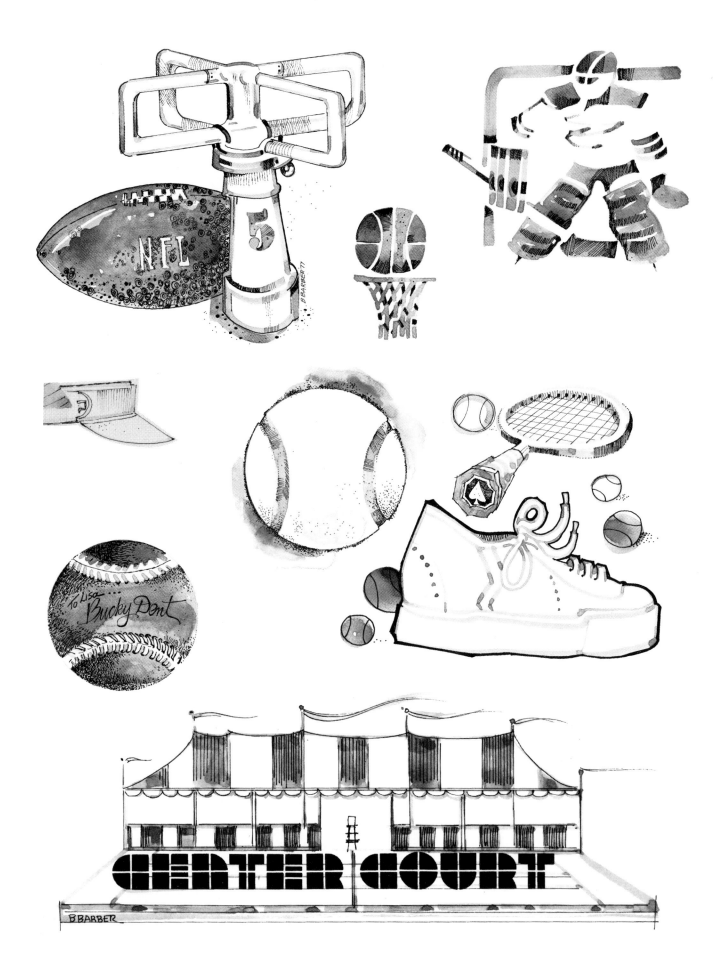

342

STUDIOS

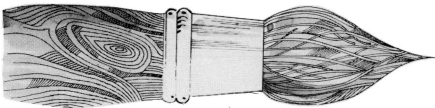

It is fitting to open this section with one of the most famous studios in this country -that of Sculptor Daniel Chester French.

Chesterwood (his studio and summer residence) is situated in an idyllic setting on 120 acres in the Berkshire Hills near Stockbridge, Massachusetts. Today, sketches, plaster casts and bronze models of French's sculpture (including the seated Lincoln and the Marite Man) can be seen at Chesterwood.

The studio's most unusual features are the railroad tracks and the 22 foot-high double doors. These elements were added to gain access to full sunlight which affects the appearance of sculptors who design work for exterior display. In 1969, Chesterwood was donated to the National Trust for Historic Preservation by Margaret French Cresson in memory of her father.

French's studio is followed by a a pair of photos used in Binney Smith's advertising campaign, featuring Racelle Strick and Jack Ceglic. The balance is an assortment of stylized studio objects, artists and interiors.

Binney Smith artists Jack Ceglic and Racelle Strick

© VOLK

© Higgins logo, Faber-Castell

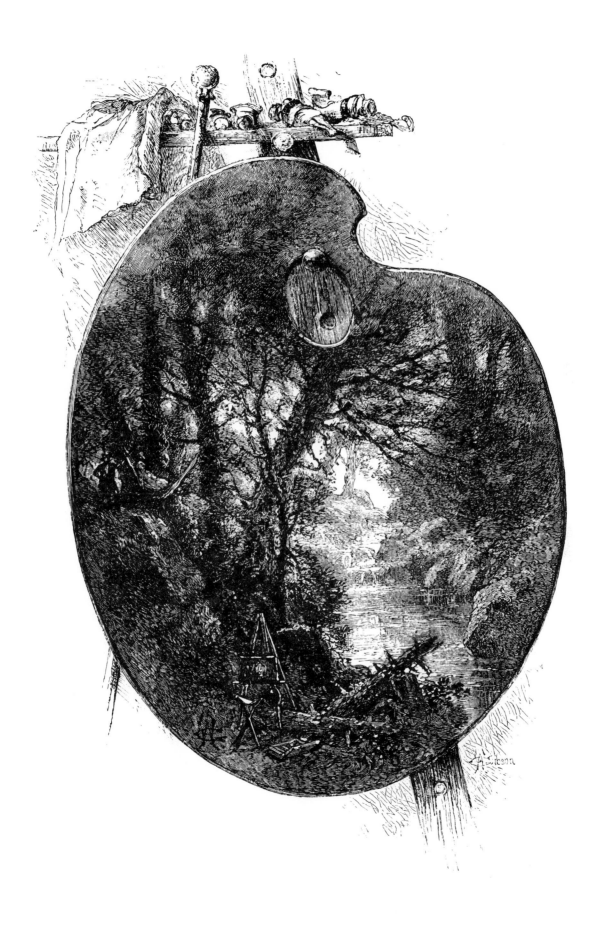

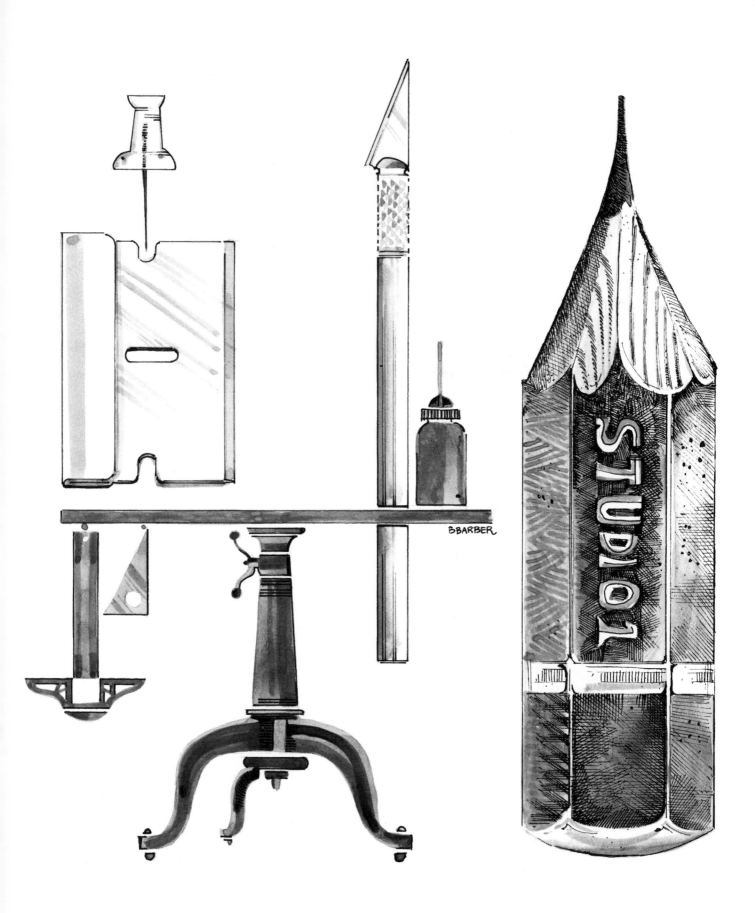

STUDIO1

BBARBER

Pitt Studios, Fred Carlson

TRADEMARKS and GRAPHICS

Trademark design is a graphic science — from the first meeting with the client to rough sketches, revisions, and mockups, to compliance with government regulations concerning ingredients, and safety in packaging, to bottle and container manufacturing. Each point is crucial, each a step closer to the final mark or package, and much has to be accomplished before a design "comes on stream."

This section begins with one of the masters, Walter Landor.

From its beginning in 1941, his firm has been recognized internationally as one of the leading advertisers serving a diversified group of small clients and multi-nationals. His better known projects include Alitalia, Singapore Airlines, Hawaiian Air, and USAir, plus work for Levis, Wells Fargo Bank, and Royal Viking Lines. Today, Mr. Landor is Chairman with John Diefenbach as President at the firm's headquarters in San

Francisco aboard the ferryboat Klamath moored at Pier 5.

The Landor work is followed by a page from the Bugdal Graphics group in Miami, a group of marks by Primo Angeli, and a page from the Olaf Gaumer firm in Frankfort, Germany.

The Appleton Machinery material is an interesting example of how one firm can design ten different logos for its internal divisions. The remaining pages contain an assortment of graphics and designs.

WELLS FARGO
BANK

CONSOLIDATED
FOODS CORPORATION

Isetan

ROYAL VIKING LINE

Landor Associates

United
National
Bank

BALDWIN

Oggo Corporation.
Fort Lauderdale, Florida,
USA.

Sails Around the World

associated paint and plastics.

AMPCO

TOBIAS, FIDLER & GOLDISS

THE BUGDAL GROUP

H.E.M.I.

Greenberg
Cuisine
International

NOAH'S ARK

The
Pasta
Factory
Company

Windjammer 'Barefoot' Cruises

GRAY DISTRIBUTION SYSTEMS

Camilo

CAMILO OFFICE FURNITURE

Bugdal Graphics

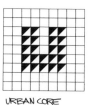

URBAN CORE

DECK HOUSE

Cone

Réa'dák

THE TOY WORKS
Middle Falls, N.Y. 12848 (518) 692-9666

Del Webb's La Posada

iBERO

combibau

MUSIK
MESSE
FRANKFURT

grill
chef

trans
parent
block

Kannemann Zeichenbedarf
Frankfurt am Main
Telefon 55 34 11 und 52 91 91
Eschersheimer Landstraße 526

layout
block

Kannemann Zeichenbedarf
Frankfurt am Main
Telefon 55 34 11 und 52 91 91
Eschersheimer Landstraße 526

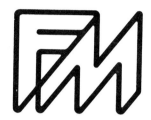

Pernionin

NAILA

DAS
STU
DIO

Art Act

DW

CHANEL

La Provence

Offsetdruck
Reproduktion
Vervielfältigung
Großfotos
Fotokopien
Microaufnahmen

Karl Michel
6056 Heusenstamm
Kreis Offenbach
Ludwigstraße 6
Telefon 06104/2446

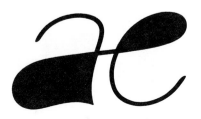

Olaf Gaumer

 Volk

 Bill Zannie

ZUM
ZUM

Appleton Machinery Co.

 CHRIST CELLA

 MADISON'S RESTAURANT & BAR

Graphics Studio

ARTICHOKES ADVERTISING
AND GRAPHIC DESIGN STUDIO
2011 K ST., N.W.☐WASH.D.C. 20006☐202/833-1600

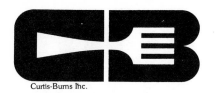
Curtis-Burns Inc.

© Buffalo

 apple® computer

THE DESIGN QUARTER, INC.

Ace-Parker

 Hotel
del
Coronado

MedailleCollege

West
Coast
Book
Warehouse

Bedfellows
The Sleeping Alternative

Cel-Art Productions

GRAPHIC INCENTIVES

Loewenstein.

LONESTAR

GRUBNEKLAF

Alvin & Company

National Watercolor Society

Note from Chuck Weber

h&tt
CHAIRS & TABLES

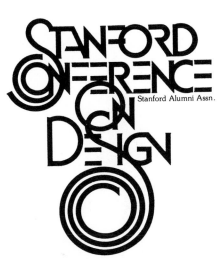
Stanford Alumni Assn.

PLAYHOUSE
ON THE SQUARE

Sandy Gorman
501 So. 13th Street
Phila. Pa. 19147
· artist ·

359

Transportation

From balloons to jets, cycles to steamboats, all the illustrations in this section relate in one way or another to the transportation scene.

Gilbert Wolin of Executive Jet Aviation will fly you anywhere in the U.S.A. for a price. The Delta Queen Steamboat Company will float you leisurely down the Mississippi on one of their grand boats — all the way to New Orleans. Ron DiCiannis' beautiful cover painting for the Rotarian magazine montages the Wright Brothers' plane at Kitty Hawk with the Great American Eagle.

Barbara Shimkus/San Antonio

360

Freelance Photographers Guild

Bombay Bicycle Club

Crow-Quill Studios for Simpson Paper

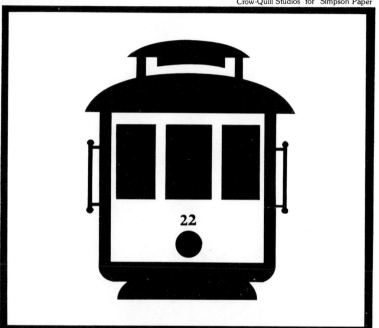

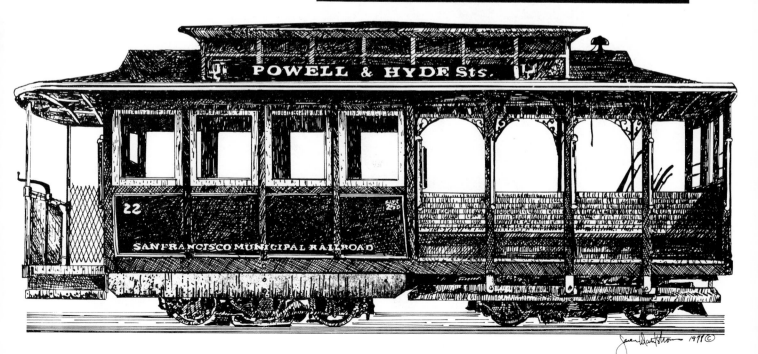

U.S.S. Constitution.

DELTA QUEEN

STEAMBOAT COMPANY

DELTA QUEEN
MISSISSIPPI QUEEN

© Pitt Studios

© Dynamics Graphics

365

31

1931 Independence
Series AE Convertible Cabriolet.

30

1930 Universal Series AD Roadster.

33

1933 Master Series
CA Sport Roadster.

CHEVROLET

Ken Dallison

winross

NEW DIMENSIONS IN COMMUNICATIONS

Metal Miniatures for Industry Premiums

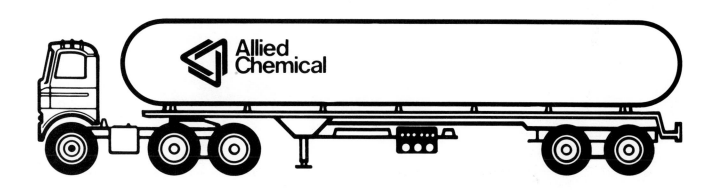

Executive Jet Aviation

Fallon Jet Corp.

Dynamic Graphics

© San Diego Convention and Visitors Bureau

The Rotarian artist Ron DiCianni

TRAVEL

As fuel costs rise, we learn that the last of the great transoceanic liners, Queen Elizabeth II, finds it hard to continue as a profit making venture. It is sad indeed to remember back when so many of the liners vied for passengers in a very competitive area of the world's oceans. With the advent of the jumbo jet, almost all of these greats are gone - the United States, the Normandie, the Queen Mary, and the Ile de France.

The smart illustration of the Queen Elizabeth II is from their around-the-world trip brochure. It is accompanied by a montage of very old and choice trunk and luggage stickers. Plying the Pacific are the fine ships of the Princess Tours. A sampling of their excellent line drawings are shown to illustrate how well designed travel ads can be used.

© Cunard

370

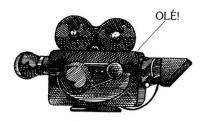

OLÉ!

PRINCESS TOURS,
THE VACATION COMPANY

371

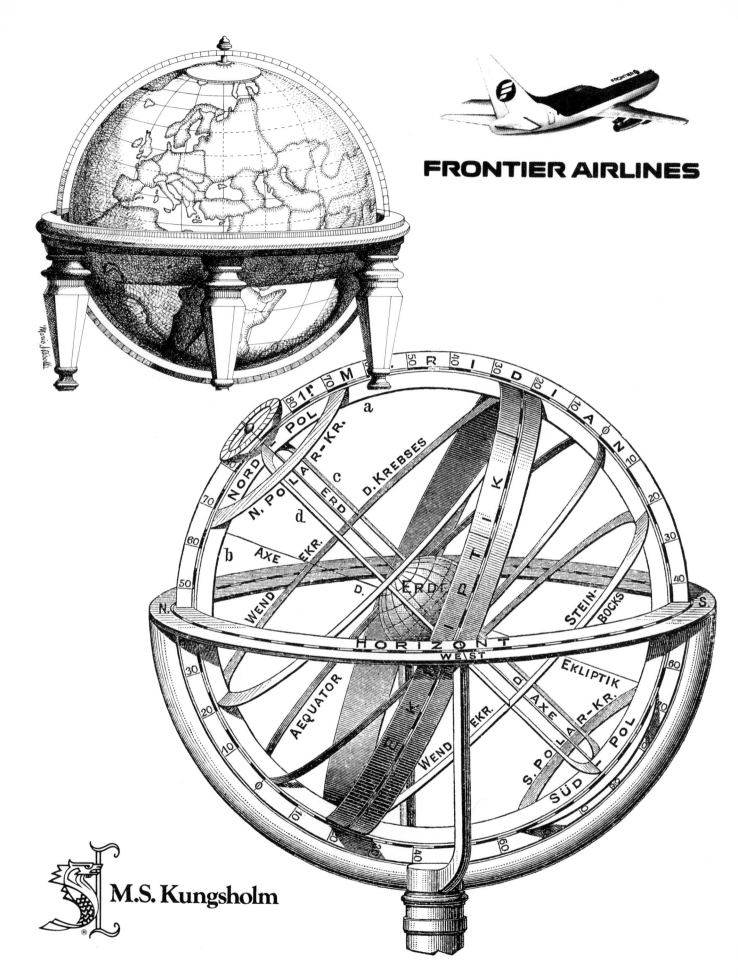

FRONTIER AIRLINES

M.S. Kungsholm

© Naiad Einsel

VALENTINES

The heart shape has been drawn, formed, painted and used more than any other, and these pages contribute to the collective effort.

The section opens with the talented Naiad Einsel and moves to an early Durer engraving, treatments by Dynamic Graphics, Volk, and the San Francisco Museum.

The Irish Tourist Board promotes LOVE in the form of heart shamrocks and Children's Design Center uses hearts in a logotype that has a real Pennsylvania Dutch influence.

Memphis Area Chamber of Commerce
Illustrator Calvin Foster

Victorian Fire-house

The inspiration for the drawing on page 380 came from a photo of an old fire station in Galena, Illinois. The beautiful brick firehouse at right is on the east side of New York and now houses a business firm. The fire engine prints are from the Donald Art Company.

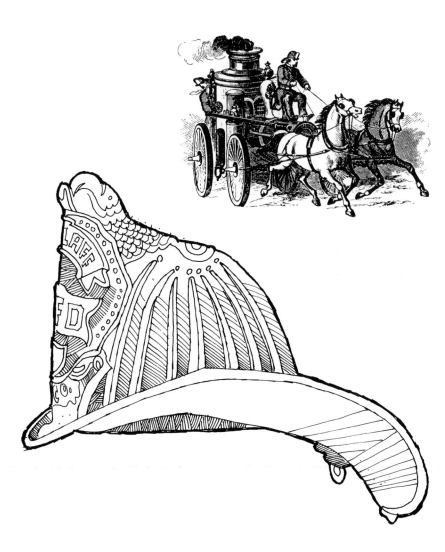

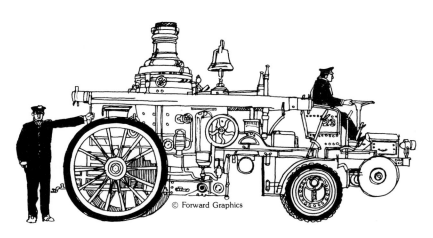

© Forward Graphics

The Western Connection

National Park Service artist Dug Waggoner

Western influences are all around us today —
boots and blue jeans stores on every corner,
mechanical bulls in saloons, and western cafes on
Manhattan Island.

Within this section are loads of western
paraphernalia, including saddles, spurs, and brands.
There is a group of Volk drawings and an excellent
photograph used by the Quaker Oats company for
their Wolf Chili advertisements.

381

Utah Travel Council

© Billy the Kid

PETER MᶜINTYRE'S

WEST

A Sunset Book

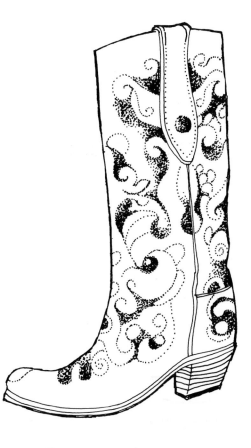

Utah Travel Council

WINES

It is interesting to see how wine firms handle their advertising. Illustration and photo techniques differ from company to company.

Christian Brothers uses company buildings as a distinct promotional symbol. The Marquis de Goulaine Muscadet ad campaign incorporates the Chateau de Goulaine in their ads, along with the ancestral lineage of the company's founders.

It is fascinating to read the Sebastiani newsletters which describe in minute detail how vineyards are planted, maintained and groomed. Other issues describe barrel marking, corkscrew suggestions and recipes to accompany their wines. Julius Wile uses a fascinating cross-hatched line drawing to illustrate Delamain Cognac.

Paul Tayl

The Christian Brothers Wine Aging Cellars, St. Helena, California

Chateau de Goulaine

INTRODUCING MARQUIS DE GOULAINE.
THE FRENCH WHITE WINE WITH A HISTORY
ALMOST AS OLD AS FRANCE ITSELF.

Schieffelin and Co.

How Wine Is Made

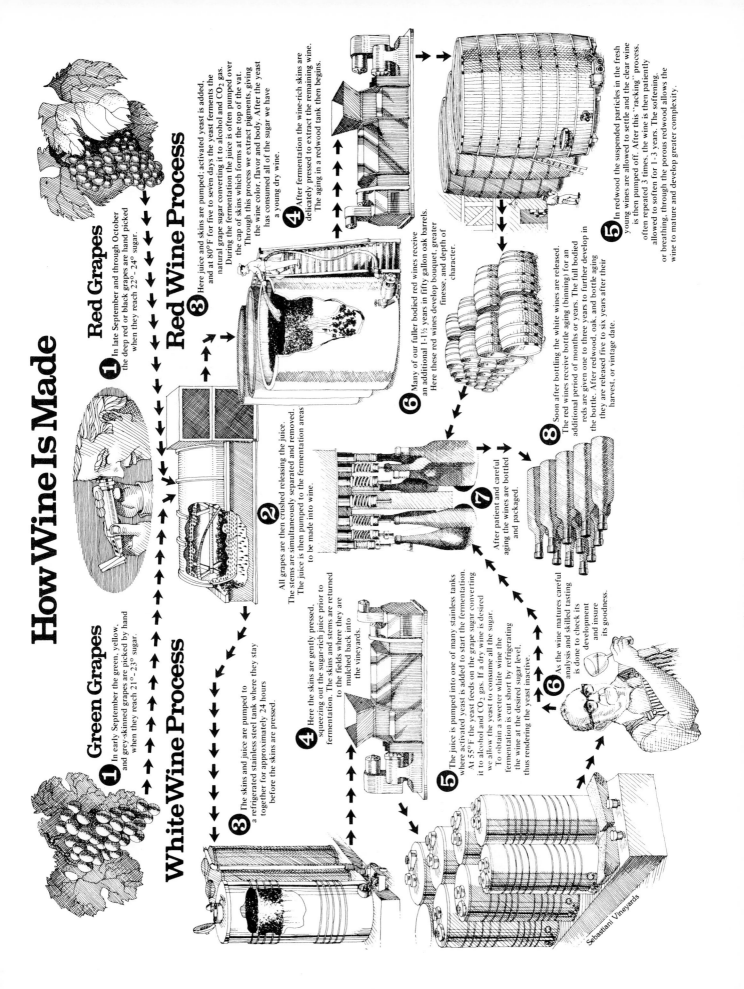

Red Grapes

1 In late September and through October the deep red or black grapes are hand picked when they reach 22°-24° sugar.

Red Wine Process

3 Here juice and skins are pumped; activated yeast is added, and at 80°F for five to seven days the yeast ferments the natural grape sugar converting it to alcohol and CO₂ gas. During the fermentation the juice is often pumped over the cap of skins which forms at the top of the vat. Through this process we extract pigments, giving the wine color, flavor and body. After the yeast has consumed all of the sugar we have a young dry wine.

4 After fermentation the wine-rich skins are delicately pressed to extract the remaining wine. The aging in a redwood tank then begins.

5 In redwood the suspended particles in the fresh young wines are allowed to settle and the clear wine is then pumped off. After this "racking" process, often repeated 3 times, the wine is patiently allowed to soften for 1-3 years. The softening, or breathing, through the porous redwood allows the wine to mature and develop greater complexity.

6 Many of our fuller bodied red wines receive an additional 1-1½ years in fifty gallon oak barrels. Here these red wines develop bouquet, greater finesse, and depth of character.

8 Soon after bottling the white wines are released. The red wines receive bottle aging (binning) for an additional period of months or years. The full bodied reds are given one to three years to further develop in the bottle. After redwood, oak, and bottle aging they are released five to six years after their harvest, or vintage date.

7 After patient and careful aging the wines are bottled and packaged.

Green Grapes

1 In early September the green, yellow, and grey-skinned grapes are picked by hand when they reach 21°-23° sugar.

White Wine Process

2 All grapes are then crushed releasing the juice. The stems are simultaneously separated and removed. The juice is then pumped to the fermentation areas to be made into wine.

3 The skins and juice are pumped to a refrigerated stainless steel tank where they stay together for approximately 24 hours before the skins are pressed.

4 Here the skins are gently pressed, squeezing out the sugar-rich juice prior to fermentation. The skins and stems are returned to the fields where they are mulched back into the vineyards.

5 The juice is pumped into one of many stainless tanks where activated yeast is added to start the fermentation. At 55°F the yeast feeds on the grape sugar converting it to alcohol and CO₂ gas. If a dry wine is desired we allow the yeast to consume all the sugar. To obtain a sweeter white wine the fermentation is cut short by refrigerating the wine at the desired sugar level, thus rendering the yeast inactive.

6 As the wine matures careful analysis and skilled tasting is done to check its development and insure its goodness.

Sebastiani Vineyards

389

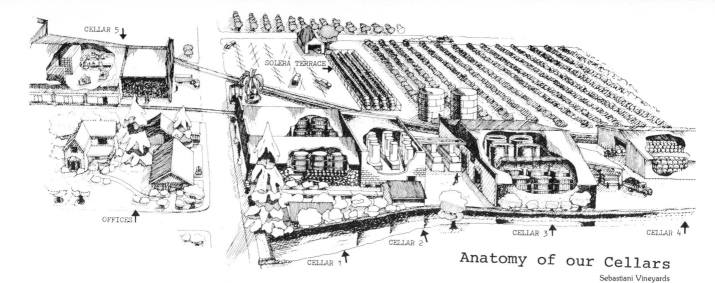

Anatomy of our Cellars

Sebastiani Vineyards

Geyser Peak Winery

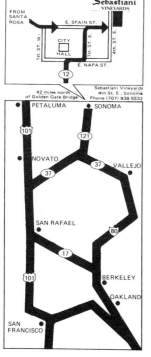

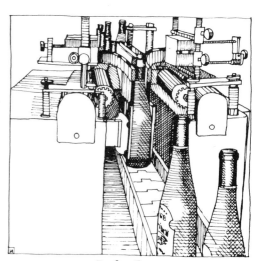

Labeler

390

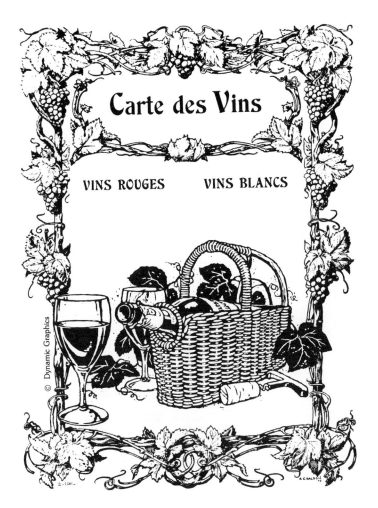

Carte des Vins

VINS ROUGES   VINS BLANCS

© Dynamic Graphics

Mirassou Wines

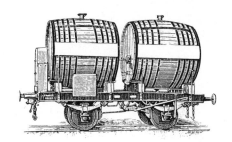

Picking by Hand

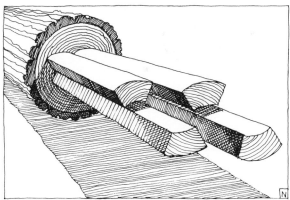

Redwood Staves

Christian Brothers

391

Heitz Cellar

Mechanical Harvester

HEAD HOOP
QUARTER HOOP
HOOP RIVET
BILGE HOOP
BUNGHOLE
BUNG STAVE
STAVE
STAVE JOINT
QUARTER HOOP
CHIME
CANT
HEAD
CROZE
HOOP PUNCH
BILGE HOOP
HOOP FASTENER
JOINT BETWEEN HEAD SECTIONS

1976
Sebastiani
PINOT NOIR BLANC

Sun Sculpture by Bruce Barber

WOOD

Wood has always been one of the finest art materials — from the early wooden churches of Kihzi (shown in the Russia section) to the imaginative work of Louise Nevelson today. It is used for carved signs, display boxes, and recycled-restored homes, among other things.

Western Wood Products Association promotes the use of wood in urban development. It can beautifully transform a drab urban area into a sparkling cityscape.

Honest Woodcarving!

The Family Handyman

The Woodsmith's STUDIO

142 East 32d Street • New York City 10016

Western Wood Products Assn.

James Arnold

gosman's fish market

Storebest Corp.

MONTAUK YACHT CLUB INN

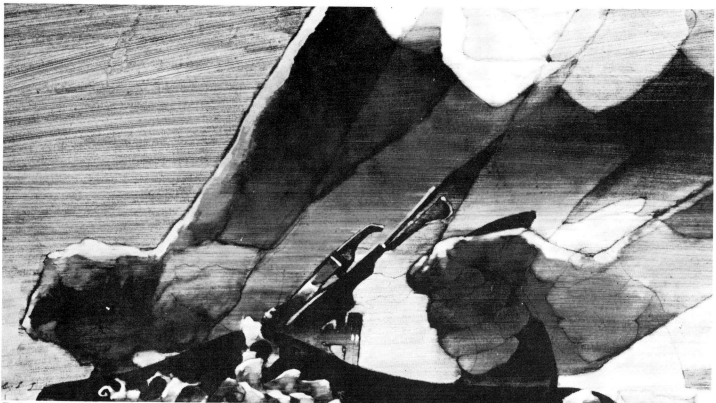

The Family Handyman

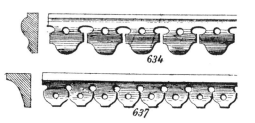

634

637

The Botticelli Piazza

Western Tri-Pack Corp.
Bendix American Forest Products Corp.

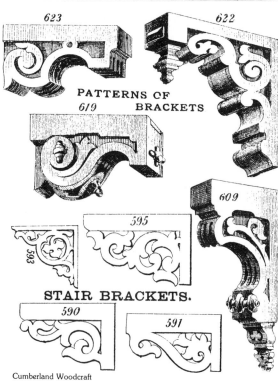

623

622

PATTERNS OF
BRACKETS

619

609

595

593

STAIR BRACKETS.

590

591

Cumberland Woodcraft

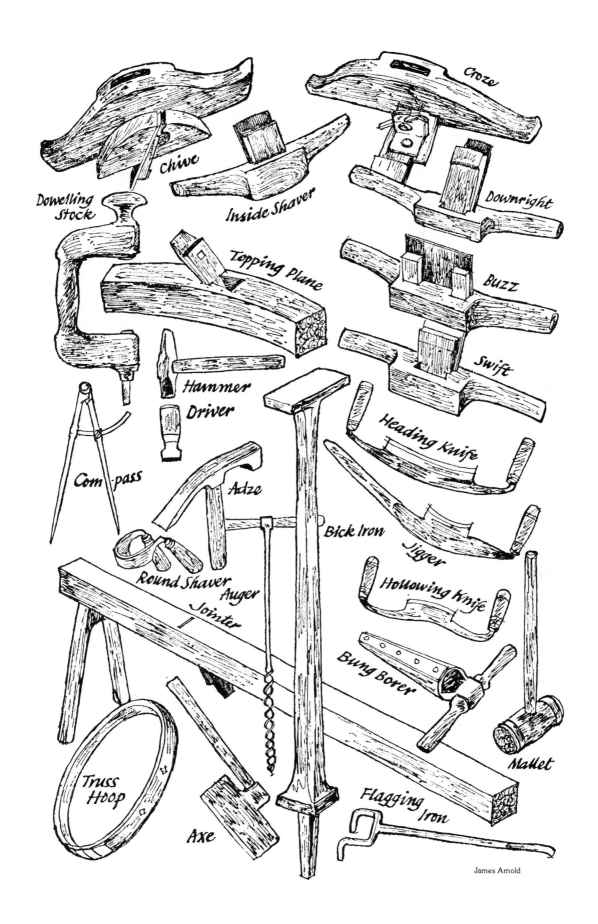

Chive

Croze

Dowelling Stock

Inside Shaver

Downright

Topping Plane

Buzz

Hammer Driver

Swift

Com-pass

Adze

Heading Knife

Round Shaver

Bick Iron

Jigger

Auger

Hollowing Knife

Jointer

Bung Borer

Mallet

Truss Hoop

Axe

Flagging Iron

James Arnold

399

Thanks to everyone who
has contributed to make this a
real workbook of ideas for
designers.

Bruce T. Barber

Credits

Animal Zoo

Canton Advertising, P.O. Box 398, Canton MA 02021 (Agency — Hills)

Einsel, Naiad, 26 Morningside Dr., South Westport CT 06880

Grit Publishing Co., Williamsport PA 17701

Hills Department Store, 15 Dan, Canton, MA 02021

Markham Park Zoo, P.O. Box 8844, Oakland Park FL 33310

Master Eagle Family of Companies, 40 W. 25th, New York NY 10010

Pitt Studios, 4 Gateway Center, Pittsburgh PA 15222

Zoological Society of San Diego, P.O. Box 551, San Diego CA 92112

Aztecs, Incas and Mayas

Barton Brands Ltd., 200 S. Michigan Ave., Chicago IL 60604

Dynamic Graphics (see Clip Services)

Freelance Photographers Guild Inc., 251 Park Ave. South, New York NY 10010

Ballooning

The Balloon Ranch, Star Rt., Del Norte CO 81132

Kew, Tony, 1 Treadgold Crescent, Don Mills, Ontario, Canada

Par Avion Inc., 361 Delaware, Buffalo NY (Agency — Finley H. Greene, 370 Franklin, Buffalo NY)

Rochester Telephone, 100 Midtown Plaza, Rochester NY 14646

Baskets

Arnold, James, Lower Egleton, Ledbury, Herefordshire England

New England Hardwood Baskets, Basketville, RR 1, Putney VT 05346

Taylor, Paul, Los Angeles CA

Bavaria

Dynamic Graphics (see Clip Services)

Folkwear Ethnic Patterns, Box 3798, San Rafael CA 94902

The Californians

Creamer/FSR, 410 N. Michigan Ave., Chicago IL 60611 (Agency — Ludowici Tiles)

Ludowici Celadon, 111 E. Wacker Dr., Chicago IL 60601

Zebot, George, 307½ 36th St., Newport Beach CA 92663

Christmas

Butte, Bruce Sr., P.O. Box 307, Jacksonville OR 97540

Design Quarter, 2900 4th Ave., San Diego CA 92103

Einsel, Naiad and Walter (see Animal)

Forstall Typographers, 1201 S. Rampart St., New Orleans LA 70153

Fortune, Time & Life Bldg., Rockefeller Center, New York NY 10020

Halls, 505 Armour Rd., N. Kansas City MO 64116

Jackson & Perkins Co., Medford OR 97501 (Agency — Harry & David)

Stasolla, Tuxedo Park, New York NY 10987 (Illustrator — Fortune Magazine)

Williams-Sonoma, P.O. Box 3792, San Francisco CA 94119

Circles

San Diego Convention and Visitors Bureau, 1200 Third Ave., San Diego CA

Volk (see Clip Services)

Cities

Atlanta Convention & Visitors Bureau, 233 Peachtree NE, Atlanta GA 30303

Baxter, Norman, 8323 Westglen, Houston TX 77063

Cincinnati Convention & Visitors Bureau, 200 W. 5th, Cincinnati OH 45202

Dallas County Heritage Society Inc., 1717 Gano, Dallas TX 75212

Frontier Airlines, 8250 Smith Rd., Denver CO 80207

Hotel Triumph Sheraton, 2737 Keele St., Toronto Canada M3M 2E9

KFWB Radio, 6230 Yucca St., Los Angeles CA 90028

Northern Kentucky Convention & Visitors Bureau, 129 E. 2nd St., Covington KY 41011

Philadelphia Convention & Visitors Bureau, 1525 JFK Blvd., Philadelphia PA 19102

Philadelphia Economic & Industrial Development Corp., One E. Penn Sq., Philadelphia PA 19107

Sive Associates, 5 W. 4th St., Cincinnati OH 45202 (Agency — Northern Kentucky Convention & Visitors Bureau)

Southland Corp., 2828 N. Haskell Ave., Dallas TX 75221

Tracy-Locke, 7503 Marin Dr., Englewood CO 80110 (Agency — Frontier Airlines)

Weller, Don, The Weller Institute, 2427 Park Oak Dr., Los Angeles CA 90068

Clip Services

American Airlines, P.O. Box 61616, DFW Airport TX 75261

Association Image Art, 12107 Nebel St., Rockville MD 20852

Board Report, P.O. Box 1561, Harrisburg PA 17105

Dynamic Graphics, 6707 N. Sheridan Rd., Peoria IL 61614

Forward Graphics, 7031 University Ave., Des Moines IA 50311

United Airlines, P.O. Box 66100, Chicago IL 60666

Volk Corporation, 1401 N. Main St., Pleasantville NJ 08232

Country

Buck Stove, West, 960 Grant St., Benicia CA 94510

Cheinco Housewares, William St., Burlington NJ 08016

Clayton, Margaret M., 6500 Burlwood Rd., Charlotte NC 28211

Einsel, Naiad (see Animal)

General Foods Corp., 250 North St., White Plains NY 10602

Hooks Drug Co., 2800 Enterprise St., Indianapolis IN 46226

Morton Salt Co., 110 N. Wacker Dr., Chicago IL 60606

Patterson's Mill Country Store, Rt. 2, Farrington Rd., Chapel Hill NC

Taylor, Paul, Los Angeles CA

Vermont Bean Seed Co., Garden Lane, Bomoseen VT 05732

England

Barbican Centre, 11 Cromwell Tower, Barbican, London England EC2Y 8DD

British Tourist Authority, 680 5th Ave., New York NY 10019

City of Edinburgh District Council, 9 Cockburn St., Edinburgh Scotland

Dynamic Graphics (see Clip Services)

Freelance Photographers Guild (see Aztecs)

Wisdom Import Sales Co., P.O. Box 18348, Irvine CA 92719

Egypt

Needham, Harper and Steers Advertising, Inc., 10889 Wilshire Blvd., Los Angeles CA 90024 (Agency for Atlantic Richfield Co.)

The First Americans

Freelance Photographers Guild (see Aztecs)

McConnell, Keith, 2131 Bonita Dr., Glendale CA 91208

Mead Printing & Writing Paper Div., Dayton OH

Rockwell-Corning Museum, Corning NY 14830

Shawmut Bank of Boston, 1 Federal St., Boston MA 02110

Volk (see Clip Services)

Food

B. Altman & Co., 361 5th Ave., New York NY 10016

Dairy Bureau of Canada, 20 Holly St., Toronto Canada M5S 2E6

First Colony Coffee & Tea Co. Inc., 204 W. 22nd St., Norfolk VA 23517

Norseland Foods, 100 Prospect, Stamford CT 06901

Ontario Pork Producers Mktg. Bd., P.O. Box 1103, Toronto Canada M6P 3K2

Potpourri Press, Box 10312, Greensboro NC 27404

Richards Group, 5350 Alpha Rd., Dallas TX 75240 (Faneuil Hall Marketplace, Boston)

Rochester Polychrome Press Inc., 45 Halstead St., Rochester NY 14610

Stavrinos, George, 76 W. 86th St., New York NY 10024

Switzerland Cheese Assn., 444 Madison Ave., New York NY 10022

United Fresh Fruit & Vegetable Assn., N. Washington, Alexandria VA 22314

France

Dairy Bureau of Canada (see Food)

Dynamic Graphics (see Clip Services)

Folkwear (see Bavaria)

Freelance Photographer Guild (see Aztecs)

Weller, Don (see Cities)

Greece

Olympic Airways, 647 Fifth Ave., New York NY 10022

Woolery Stone Co., Bloomington IN 47401

Hollandaze

Freelance Photographers Guild (see Aztecs)

Province of Ontario, Ministry of Tourism, Queens Park, Toronto Canada M7A 2E5

Ice Cream Parlors

Coca-Cola Company, P.O. Drawer 1734, Atlanta GA 30301

Letraset USA Inc., 40 Eisenhower Dr., Paramus NJ 07652

Mead Printing Paper, Dayton OH

NBC Television Stations Div., Merchandise Mart Plaza, Chicago IL 60654

Illustrators

Baxter, Norman (see Cities)

BBDO, 383 Madison Ave., New York NY 10017 (Agency — Hammermill/General Electric)

Butte, Bruce (see Cities)

Conklin, Labs & Bebee Inc., Box 4871 GM Circle, Syracuse NY 13221 (Agency — Oneida National Bank)

Dallison, Ken, RR 3, Indian River, Ontario Canada K0L 2B0

Einsel, Naiad (see Animal)
Folkwear (see Bavaria)
Gaadt, George, 888 Thorn St., Sewickly PA 15143
Galloway, Nick, 5455 Wilshire Blvd., Los Angeles
    CA 90036
Gray & Rogers Inc., 1234 Market St., Philadelphia PA
    19107 (Agency — Weyerhaeuser)
Hammermill Papers Group, Erie PA 16533
Hatfield, Cabell T., 264 E. Broadway, New York NY
    10002
Kamifuji, Tom, 125 University Ave., Palo Alto CA
    94301
KR Advertising, 88 Main St., Bloomsburg NJ 08804
    (Agency — Koh-I-Noor)
McConnell, Keith (see First Americans)
Moreau, Alain, 1461½ South Beverly Dr., Los
    Angeles CA 90035
Mariani, David, 4357 Chestnut Ridge Rd., Tonawanda
    NY 14150
Pitt Studios (see Animal)
Richards, Linda, 15 Cody Ave., Glenhead NY 11545
Sakahara, Dick, 28826 Cedarbluff Dr., Rancho Palos
    Verdes CA 90274
Sherrill Co., 5115 McKinney, Dallas TX 75205
    (Agency — Airport Marina Hotel)
Southwestern Bell, 1010 Pike St., St. Louis MO 63101
Taylor, Paul, Los Angeles CA
Unruh, Jack, 7616 LBJ, Dallas TX
Walker, David & Averil, 9 Learmouth Gardens,
    Edinburgh Scotland
Weller Institute (see Cities)
Weyerhaeuser Co. Paper Div., Plymouth Meeting PA
    19462
Zebot, George (see Californians)

India

Air India, 400 Park Street, New York NY 10022
Incentive Travel Magazine, 825 S. Barrington Ave.,
    Los Angeles CA 90049
India Government Tourist Office, 30 Rockefeller Plaza,
    New York NY 10020

The Islands

Livingstone Evans Enterprises, P.O. Box 64276, Los
    Angeles CA 90064
Pacific Area Travel Assn., 228 Grant Ave., San
    Francisco CA 94108
Polynesian Cultural Center, 2222 Kalakava Ave.,
    Honolulu HI 96815

Ireland

Irish Tourist Board, Box 1200, Long Island NY 11101
Gray & Rogers (Agency — Weyerhaeuser) (see
    Illustrators)
Weyerhaeuser Co. Paper Div. (see Illustrators)

Malls and Markets

Citicorp Center, 53rd & Lexington, New York NY
    10043

Embarcadero Center, 3 Embarcadero Center, San
    Francisco CA 94111
Freight House Shops, Smithfield & West Carson,
    Pittsburgh PA 15222
Ghirardelli Square, 900 N. Point St., San Francisco
    CA 94109
Harborplace, 553 World Trade Center, Baltimore MD
    21201
Newmarket, Philadelphia PA
Olla Podrida, 12215 Coit Rd., Dallas TX 75230
Pier 39, P.O. Box 3730, San Francisco CA 94119
Richards Group (see Food)
    (Agency — Faneuil Hall Marketplace, Boston)
The Rouse Co., Columbia MD 21044
Saint Peters Church, 619 Lexington, New York NY
    10022
Slotnick's Daughter, Citicorp Center, 153 E. 53rd St.,
    New York NY 10022
Schenck, Plunk & Deason, Two North Park East,
    Dallas TX 75231 (Agency — Olla Podrida)

Maple Syrup

International Maple Syrup Institute, 643 Grosvenor,
    Montreal, Quebec Canada H3Y 2S9
Ontario Maple Producers Assn., Ontario Food Council,
    1200 Bay St., Toronto Canada M7A 2B2
Ontario Ministry of Agriculture and Food — Maple
    Syrup Extension, Elmvale, Ontario Canada L0L 1P0

The Market at Marrakesh

Mataam Fez Moroccan Restaurant, 4609 E. Colfax,
    Denver CO 80220

Mexico

Barrington Publications Inc.
Estebans, 903 Marquette, Minneapolis MN 55402
Mexican Government Tourism Office, 9701 Wilshire
    Blvd., Beverly Hills CA 90212

Mills, Grains and Bread

Baxter, Norman (see Cities)
Bel-Art Advertising, 6211 Lemmon, Dallas TX
    75221
Bloomingdale's, 1000 Third Ave., New York NY
Forward Graphics (see Clip Services)
Greif Brothers, 1821 University Ave., St. Paul MN
    55104
Nelson L.B. Corp., 64 Willow Pl., Menlo Park CA
    94025 (Old Mill Shopping Mall)
Original Spool Furniture Co., P.O. Box 16063,
    Houston TX 77022
Spaulding & Frost, Fremont NH 03044
Wausau Papers, Brokaw WI 54417

Office Equipment

Alling & Cory, 25 Verona, Rochester NY 14602
Beckett Paper Co., The, Hamilton OH 45012
Brewer, Jones & Feldman, Inc., 7507 Reading Rd.,
    Cincinnati OH 45237 (Agency — Beckett Paper)

Colossus Corp., P.O. Box 680, New Haven CT 06503
Group Four Mail, Inc., 15 E. Bethpage Rd., Plainview NY 11803
Pitney-Bowes, Walnut and Pacific Streets, Stamford CT 06904
Salisbury, Mike, 2237 Stanley Hills Dr., Los Angeles CA 90046

Oil

City Investing Co., 767 Fifth Ave., New York NY 10022
Esmark Inc., 55 E. Monroe St., Chicago IL 60603
Hardware Age Magazine, Chilton Way, Radnor PA 19089
Texaco Inc., 2000 Westchester Ave., White Plains NY 10650
Volk (see Clip Services)
Westinghouse-Lamp Commercial Div., Bloomfield NJ 07003

Orient Express

B. Altman and Co. (see Food)
Gerber Advertising Agency, 1305 Southwest 12th Ave., Portland OR 97201
Han Syi Studio, 34 Main St., Tiburon CA 94920
Hengerer, The William Co., 465 Main St., Buffalo NY 14203
Hong Kong Tourist Assn., 160 Sansome St., San Francisco CA
Horikawa Restaurants, Tokyo, Los Angeles, Santa Ana
International Paper Co., P.O. Box 8411, Portland OR 97207
Japan Inn Inc., 1715 Wisconsin Ave., Washington D.C. 20007
Japan Air Lines, 655 Fifth Ave., New York NY 10022
Japan National Tourist Organization, 45 Rockefeller Plaza, New York NY 10020
Japan Society, 333 E. 47th St., New York NY 10017
Liu, Y.J. c/o Diane Liu, 83 Corte Placida, Greenbrae CA 94904
Rotarian Magazine, 1600 Ridge Ave., Evanston IL 60201
Taylor & NG, 480 Ninth St., San Francisco CA 94103

Outerbanks

Atlantic Associates, Ramada Inn Suite 120, 50 Dayton, Danvers MA 01923
Blish, Carolyn, artist — S.T. Preston & Sons
Freelance Photographers Guild (see Aztecs)
Gourmet Magazine, 777 Third Ave., New York NY 10017
Hatfield, Cabell (see Illustrators)
John de Graff Inc., Clinton Corners NY 12514 (Publisher — The Marlinspike Sailor)
Kimric Products, 678 Washington St., Lynn MA 01901
Mystic Seaport, Mystic CT 06355
Preston, S.T. & Sons, Main St. Wharf, Greenport L.I. NY 11944
Sea Pines Plantation Co., Hilton Head SC 29948
Smith, Hervey Garrett (author — The Marlinspike Sailor)

Recycled Buildings

Adgraphics, 632 City Park Ave., Columbus OH 43206 (Agency — Renaissance, Olentangy Management Co.)
Butte, Bruce (see Christmas)
Cumberland Woodcraft Co., RD #5, Rural Box 452, Carlisle PA 17013
Finch, Pruyn & Co. Inc., Glens Falls NY 12801
Focal Point, 3760 Lower Roswell Rd., Marietta GA 30060
Golden Movement Emporium, 2821 Main St., Santa Monica CA 90405
Heritage Place, 44 Gough St., San Francisco CA 94103
Livingstone Evans Enterprises (see Islands)
Mary Rae & Associates Ltd., 950 Logan St., Denver CO 80203
National Trust for Historic Preservation, 1785 Massachusetts Ave. NW, Washington D.C. 20036
Olentangy Management Co., 1265 Neil Ave., Columbus OH 43201
Prince of Wales Hotel, The, Niagara on the Lake, Canada
San Francisco Victoriana, 2245 Palou St., San Francisco CA 94124
Thompson, Kenneth J., 2239 Sutton Rd., York PA 17403 (Agency — Cumberland)
Trolley Square, 7 E. 5th South, Salt Lake City UT 84102
Welsbach Lighting, 3001 E. Madison St., Baltimore MD 21205

Restaurants

Ad-Com, 10800 Lyndale Ave., S., Bloomington MN 55420 (Agency — Harry Sheldons)
Arnold & Co., 2221 S. Fillmore Observatory Park, Denver CO 80210 (Agency — Mataam-Fez)
Austin Kelly Advertising, 880 Johnson Ferry Rd. N.E., Atlanta GA 30342 (Agency — Nikolai's Roof)
Beque's, Royal Sonesta, New Orleans LA
Best Western Las Palmas Inn, 6233 Int'l. Dr., Orlando FL 32809
Boojum Tree, 205 Strander Blvd., Seattle WA 98188
Bowes/Hanlon, 550 Pharr Rd. N.E., Atlanta GA 30305 (Agency — W.D. Crowley's)
Brown, Ida, 2201 Leavenworth, San Francisco CA 94133 (Agency — Ernie's)
Carlton Advertising, 925 Penn Ave., Pittsburgh PA 15222 (Agency — The Salad Co.)
Ciao, 230 Jackson St., San Francisco CA 94111
Cisco's Cafe, 1964 Winchester Rd., Memphis TN 38116
Crackers, 2621 McKinney, Dallas TX 75204
Crowley's, W.D. (see Ad-Com)
Design Publications, 717 5th Ave., New York NY 10022 (Industrial Design Mag. — Healthworks Photos)
Dock of the Bay, 235 University Ave., Berkeley Marina, Berkeley CA 94710
Dynamic Graphics (see Clip Services)

Harpenau Enterprises, 8001 Reading Rd., Cincinnati OH 45237 (Agency — La Ronde)

Healthworks, 1290 Ave. of the Americas, New York NY 10019

Jethro's - Jasons Food & Spirits, 1499 W. Palmetto Park Rd., Boca Raton FL 33432

Juniors Restaurant (see Levison & Sacks) Miami FL

Kelly's of Mole St., 1620 Ludlow, Philadelphia PA 19103

La Ronde Restaurant, 8001 Reading Rd., Cincinnati OH 45237

Levison & Sacks Adv., 9400 S. Dadeland Blvd., Miami FL 33156

Luchow's, 110 E. 14th St., New York NY 10003

Maison Gerard, 224 S. Beverly Dr., Beverly Hills CA

Matne 2, 228 Valencia, Coral Gables FL 33134 (Agency — Tuttle's)

Mr. Greenjeans, 354 King St. E., Toronto Canada M5A 1K9

More & Assoc., 833 Conti St., New Orleans LA 70112 (Agency — Begue's)

One Hundred and One Productions, 834 Mission St., San Francisco CA 94103

Paxson Advertising, Landmark Bldg., San Antonio TX 78205 (Agency — Shuckers)

Peterson Associates, 1314 S. Kivy, Honolulu HA 96814 (Agency — Whales Tale)

Piret's, 4901 Morena Blvd., San Diego CA 92117

Putsch's, 300 W. 47th St., Kansas City MO 64112

Razidlo Advertising, 2105 1st Ave. S., Minneapolis MN 55404 (Agency — 510)

Seventeen Eighty Nine, 1226 Thirty-Sixth St. N.W., Washington D.C. 20007

Sausalito, The, 1216 N. La Salle, Chicago IL 60610

Shuckers Restaurant, San Antonio TX

Sievers, Lee & Mary, 5516 Queen Ave. S., Minneapolis MN 55410 (Agency — Harry Sheldons)

Signature Magazine, 260 Madison Ave., New York NY 10016 (artist — Dick Sommers)

Spectrum Foods Inc., Pier 1, San Francisco CA 94111

St. Orres Inn, P.O. Box 523, Gualala CA 95445

Stockman, Judith, 1270 Ave. of the Americas, New York NY 10020 (Agency — Luchow's)

Stouffer's Surf Hotel, 440 Sea Breeze, Ft. Lauderdale FL 33316

Trombetta & Youngs Enterprises, 2800 Leavenworth, San Francisco CA 94133 (Harpos — Management)

Unruh, Jack (see Illustrators)

Whales Tale, 666 Front St., Lahaina, Maui HA 69761

Windows on the World (Inhilco Inc.), 106th Fl., World Trade Center, New York NY 10048

Wyse Advertising, 2800 Euclid Ave., Cleveland OH 44115 (Agency — Cheese Cellar, Top of the Surf)

Retail Serendipity

Barrett Hill Inc., 160 E. 56th St., New York NY 10022

Bergdorf Goodman, 754 5th Ave., New York NY 10019

Crate & Barrel, 190 Northfield Rd., Northfield IL 60093

Dansk International Designs Ltd., Mt. Kisco NY 10549

Gloria Vanderbilt for Murjani USA Ltd., 498 7th Ave., New York NY 10018

Greater Newbury Port Chamber of Commerce, 29 State St., Newbury Port MA 01950

Greetings Magazine, 95 Madison Ave., New York NY 10016

Hengerer, The Wm. Co. (see Orient Express)

North Park Merchants Assn., 1030 North Park, Dallas TX 75225

Richards, Linda (see Illustrators)

Toni Totes, So. Londonderry VT 05155

Walcher, Laura, 3752 Vista de la Bahia, San Diego CA 92117 (Agency — Bazaar del Mondo)

Russia

Folkwear (see Bavaria)

Pullman Inc., 200 S. Michigan, Chicago IL 60604

Silhouette

Amsted Industries, 3700 Prudential Plaza, Chicago IL 60601

Dancer Fitzgerald Sample Inc., 1010 Battery St., San Francisco CA 94111

Esmark Inc. (see Oil)

Habersham Plantation, P.O. Box 1209, Toccoa GA 30577

Live Steam, P.O. Box 286, Cadillac MI 49601

Nicholson Design, 1950 5th Ave., San Diego CA 92101 (Agency/Designer — Pacific Builders)

Outdoor Traders Inc., 79 E. Putnam Ave., Greenwich CT 06830

Pacific Coast Builders Conference Inc., 235 Montgomery, San Francisco CA 94104

Pittsburgh Hyatt House, Pittsburgh PA 15219

Simmons, Marvin, Lehigh University, Bethlehem PA 18015

Taylor & Mathis, 10 Perimeter Center East N.E., Atlanta GA 30338

Western Airlines, P.O. Box 92005, World Way Postal Center, Los Angeles CA 90009

Sports

American Mutual Liability Insurance Co., Wakefield MA 01880

Artmaster, 133 Chenoweth Lane, Louisville KY 40207

Aspen Skiing Corp., Box 1248, Aspen CO 81611

BBDO (see Illustrators)

Bauer, Eddie, 1737 Airport Way South, Seattle WA 98134

Meadowlands Hilton Hotel, The, 2 Harmon Pl., Secaucus NJ 07094

Minneapolis/St. Paul Magazine, 512 Nicollet Mall, Minneapolis MN 55402

New York Telephone, 1095 Ave. of the Americas, New York NY

Snowmass, Box 5566, Snowmass Resort CO 81615

Studios

Binney Smith, 1100 Church Lane, Easton PA 18042
Chesterwood, P.O. Box 248, Stockbridge MA 01262
Grumbacher, 460 W. 34th St., New York NY 10001
James Neal Harvey, 477 Madison Ave., New York NY 10022 (Agency — Binney Smith)
Pitt Studios (see Animal)
Wills Grant Marketing Communications Inc., 275 S. 19th St., Philadelphia PA 19103 (Agency — Faber-Castell Higgins)
Winsor & Newton, 555 Winsor Dr., Secaucus NJ 07094

Trademarks and Graphics

Ace-Parker, 3850 N.W. 30th Ave., Miami FL 33142
Anaheim Visitor & Convention Bureau, 800 N. Katella, Anaheim CA 92802
American Business Press Inc., 205 E. 42nd St., New York NY 10017
Apple Computer Inc., 10260 Bandley Dr., Cupertino CA 95014
Appleton Machine Co., Appleton WI 54913
Artichokes Advertising, 2011 K St., N.W., Washington D.C.
Beasley Company, 1847 W. Alabama, Houston TX 77098
Briar Patch, The, 867 Grand Ave., St. Paul MN 55102
Bruce, Henry & Davis, 10688 Haddington, Houston TX 77043 (Agency — Best Broncos of Texas)
Butler County Mushroom Farm, Worthington PA 16262
Bugdal Graphics, 7227 NW 7th St., Miami FL 33126
California Iceberg Lettuce Commission, P.O. Box 3354, Monterey CA 93940
Canadian National, P.O. Box 8100, Montreal, Quebec Canada H3C 3N4
Cel-Art Productions, 7 E. 48th St., New York NY 10017
Christ Cella, 160 E. 46th St., New York NY 10017
Ckat & Associates Inc., 103 Plandome Rd., Manhasset NY 11030
Cone Mills Marketing Co., 1440 Broadway, New York NY 10018
Corporate Communications, Pacific Trade Center, Honolulu HA 96813 (Agency — Poipu Kai)
Creative Express, 551 Franklin, Buffalo NY 14202 (Agency — Tennis Unlimited)
Curtis-Burns Inc, 1 Lincoln First Sq., Rochester NY 14602
Deck House Inc., 930 Main St., Acton MA 01720
Design Quarter (see Christmas)
DBG&H Ltd., 2451 Stemmons, Dallas TX 75207 (Agency — Madison)
Gaumer, Olaf, 6 Frankfurt Am Main, Holzhausen Strasse 2 Germany
Gorman, Sandy, 501 S. 13th St., Philadelphia PA 19147
Grub-ne-Klaf, 255 Colrain Rd., Greenfield MA 01301
Graphics Studio, 8721 Beverly, Los Angeles CA 90048

Graphic Incentives, P.O. Box, Colorado Springs CO 80901
Jack Douglas & Associates Inc., 9999 Richmond Ave., Houston TX 77042
Landor Associates, Ferryboat Klamath, Pier 5, San Francisco CA 94111
La Posada, 4949 E. Lincoln Dr., Scottsdale AZ 85253
Loewenstein, Hank Inc., 3260 SW 11 Ave., Fort Lauderdale FL 33335
May, Robert, 251 Corona St., Rosemere, Quebec Canada J7A 2P4
National Watercolor Society, 628 San Diegurto Dr., Encinitas CA 92024
Quail Ridge, Box 1806, Delray Beach FL 33444
Restaurant Associates Industries, 1540 Broadway, New York NY 10036 (Agency — Zum Zum)
Sioux Falls Dept. of Commercial Development, 100 N. Phillips Ave., Sioux Falls SD 57102
Toy Works, The, Middle Falls NY 12848
The Committee, 3620 Fredonia, Hollywood CA 90068 (Agency — Bedfellows)
Unigraphics Inc., 2905 Maple Ave., Dallas TX 75201
Vanderbyl, Michael, 1000 Sansome St., San Francisco CA 94111
Visual Merchandising Show of Calif., 27 Scott St., San Francisco CA 94117 (Designer — M. Vanderbyl)
West Coast Book Warehouse, 1920 Main St., Forest Grove OR 97116
Zannie, William, 21 Colvin, Buffalo NY 14216

Transportation

B & T Fuller Bus Co., 128 E. Summit, San Antonio TX 78212
Executive Jet Aviation, Port Columbus Int'l. Airport, Columbus OH 43219
Falcon Jet Corporation, Teterboro Airport NJ 07608
Northlich, Stolley, Inc., 200 W. Fourth St., Cincinnati OH 45202
Rotarian, The, 1600 Ridge Ave., Evanston IL 60201
Shimkus, Barbara, 7930 Broadway, San Antonio TX 78209 (Agency — B & T Fuller Bus)
Winross, Box 422, Rochester NY 14602

Travel

Cole & Weber, 1619 Terry, Seattle WA 98101 (Agency — Princess Tours)
Cunard, 555 5th Ave., New York NY 10017
Flagship Cruises/M. S. Kungsholm, 522 Fifth Ave., New York NY 10036

Valentines

Children's Design Center, Geyser Rd., R.D. 4, Saratoga Springs NY 12866
Dynamic Graphics (see Clip Services)
Einsel, Naiad (see Animal)
Irish Tourist Board (see Ireland)
Memphis Area Chamber of Commerce, P.O. Box 224, Memphis TN 38101
San Francisco Museum of Art, San Francisco CA

Sliker, Julie & Roger Design Associates, 3140 Pleasant
  Grove Terrace, N.E., Grand Rapids MI 49505
  (Designers — Children's Design Center)
Volk (see Clip Services)
Walker & Associates Inc., 2605 Nonconnah Blvd.,
  Memphis TN 38132 (Agency — Memphis Area
  Chamber of Commerce)

Victorian Firehouse

Donald Art Co., 90 South Ridge St., Port Chester
  NY 10573

The Western Connection

Austin Chamber of Commerce, 901 W. Riverside,
  Austin TX 78767
Billy the Kid, 4171 N. Mesa St., El Paso TX 79988
Burry Division, Quaker Oats Co., P.O. Box 484,
  Elizabeth NJ 07207
Denver Convention & Visitors Bureau,
  225 W. Colfax, Denver CO 80202
Lane Publishing Co., Sunset Books, Willow and
  Middlefield Rds., Menlo Park CA 94025
Quaker Oats Co., The, 717 Pennsylvania Ave.,
  Elizabeth NJ 07201
United States Dept. of the Interior, Nat'l. Park Service,
  450 Golden Gate Ave., San Francisco CA 36063
Venture Tours of the West, 1123 S.W. Washington,
  Portland OR 97205
Waggoner, Dug (U.S. Dept. of Interior)
Wells Fargo Bank, 464 California St., San Francisco
  CA 94144
Utah Travel Council, Council Hall, State Capitol, Salt
  Lake City UT 84114

Wines

Buena Vista Winery Inc., 18000 Old Winery Rd.,
  Sonoma CA 95476
Christian Brothers, The, P.O. Box 420, Napa CA
  94558
Della Femina, Travisano & Partners Inc., 625 Madison
  Ave., New York NY 10022 (Agency — Schieffelin)
Geyser Peak Advertising, 4340 Redwood Hwy., San
  Rafael CA 94930
Geyser Peak Winery, Geyserville CA 95441
Heublein Inc., 601 Fourth St., San Francisco CA
  94107
Robert Mondavi Winery, P.O. Box 106, Oakville CA
  94562
Paul Masson Vineyards, P.O. Box 97, Saratoga CA
  95070
Schieffelin & Co., 30 Cooper Sq., New York NY
  10003
Sebastiani Vineyards Inc., 389 4th St., East Sonoma
  CA 95476
Sonoma Vineyards, Windsor, Sonoma County CA
  95476
Simi Winery, P.O. Box 946, Healdsburg CA 95448
Taylor, Paul, Los Angeles CA
Taylor Wine Co. Inc., The, Hammondsport NY 14840
Wile, Julius Sons & Co., New Hyde Park NY

Wood

American Box Div. - Bendix American Forest
  Products, 2740 Hyde St., San Francisco CA 94119
Arnold, James (see Baskets)
Hallelujah Redwood Products, 39500 Comptehe Rd.,
  Mendocino CA 95460
Handyman, The Family, 1999 Shepard Rd., St. Paul
  MN 55116
Honest Woodcarving!, S. Elroy Dr., Montauk NY
  11954
Montauk Signcarving Co., 75 Accabonac Rd., E.
  Hampton NY 11937
Storebest Corp., 38-56 Long Ave., Hillsdale NJ 07205
Taunton Press, The, 52 Church Hill Rd., Newtown
  CT 06470
Western Tri-Pack Corp., 330 Corey Way S., San
  Francisco CA
Western Wood Products Assn., 1500 Yeon Bldg.,
  Portland OR 97204
Woodsmiths Studio, 142 E. 32nd St., New York NY
  10016

1